DANGEROUS LANDING

Dangerous Landing

A first-hand story of evasion

HENRY ORD ROBERTSON, DFM

Foreword
by

Group Captain Leonard Cheshire
VC, OM, DSO**, DFC, RAF (Retd)

A William Kimber book
published by

PATRICK STEPHENS LIMITED

First published in 1989

British Library Cataloguing in Publication Data

Robertson, Henry Ord
Dangerous landing : a first-hand story
of evasion.
1. World War 2. Air operation by Great
Britain. Royal Air Force Bomber Command.
Biographies
I. Title
940.54'4941'0924

ISBN 1-85260-254-6

*Patrick Stephens Limited is part of the
Thorsons Publishing Group,
Wellingborough, Northamptonshire,
NN8 2RQ, England.*

Photoset in North Wales by
Derek Doyle & Associates Mold, Clwyd
and Printed in Great Britain by
Mackays of Chatham, Kent.

1 3 5 7 9 10 8 6 4 2

Contents

		Page
	Foreword by Group Captain Leonard Cheshire VC, OM, DSO, DFC, RAF (Retd)	9
	Author's Dedication	11
	Acknowledgements	13
	Introduction	15
1	Target Mannheim	19
2	Death of a Halifax	30
3	A Lucky Contact	44
4	The Cherrier Family	57
5	A Not So 'Safe House'	65
6	Next Stop Paris	90
7	Strange Hideouts	100
8	Monique	113
9	Crossing the Demarcation Line	132
10	Pat O'Leary	142
11	Disaster in the Pyrenees	154
	Appendices	167
	Index	171

List of Illustrations

Between pages 64-65
At Blackpool whilst on preliminary training
At Blackpool
Fernard Cherrier and his family after the war
Fernard Cherrier and his wife and children
The Cherriers on a visit to England in 1960
Monsieur Jean Ançelot, cure of St Julien
Monsieur Ançelot's house where the author was hidden
Odette Mailland
The café in rue St Claude, Paris
Monsieur Roussel outside his home
With Yves Chardac after the war
Gaston Denivelle in the courtyard of his home
Gaston Denivelle
Renee Denivelle

Between pages 96-97
Warning posters against harbouring enemy servicemen
With Monique Spiquel in the rue Perronet
Pat O'Leary
Certificate issued to the author in Spain
The author about 1948
Annual camp at Waddington, 1966
The graves of Pilot Officer Hillier and Sergeant Smith
Graveside ceremony at Courouvre
The author at Revigny in 1986

List of illustrations in the text

Page

Fernand Cherrier's interpretation of the action on the
    night of 6 December 1942   51
Fernand Cherrier's letter to the author after the
    Liberation   63
Odette's letter to the author   85
Author's evasion route through France   93
Allied aircraft shot down in the Meuse region, 1939-45   166

Foreword

by

Group Captain Leonard Cheshire, VC, OM, DSO**, DFC, RAF (Retd)

'The swallows have returned'
– radio message requested by the French Resistance
to announce the author's safe arrival home.

Today, just as I was collecting my thoughts to write these few words, I looked out of the window and saw that the first swallows of summer had arrived. To watch them winging their way around their once-familiar haunts, so effortlessly and so swiftly, one would hardly believe that they had just completed a 6,000-miles journey. Still less are we able to understand what inner force or secret it is that enables them to accomplish such a remarkable feat.

By the same token, I do not think that we know much about the experience of World War II aircrew who, having been shot down over enemy-occupied territory, evaded capture or else escaped from prison camp and finally made their way home to England. On two occasions, this happened to someone on my own station, both of whom we thought had been killed; and I can still today vividly remember our astonishment and our joy when they suddenly reappeared in the mess. It was noticeable that, in neither case, did the person involved want to disclose more than the bare facts of what had happened.

Although it was generally understood that there was a duty to try, escape from inside the depths of Fortress Europe involved formidable difficulties and called for unusual inner strength, self-discipline and initiative, and so could be possible only to a small minority. Even then, success was achieved at a heavy cost, not just to the evaders themselves but perhaps even more to the many French, Belgian, Dutch and other men and women who formed the escape network, knowing full well that if they were caught they would pay with their own lives; indeed, a great many did. The heroism shown by the Resistance was of the highest order, and I hope that we in Britain will never forget the debt we owe them.

This is an absorbing account of an extraordinary venture and a worthy tribute to the courage and resourcefulness of the many aircrew who tried to make it home and of those, all across Occupied Europe, who took them 'under their wing' and helped them to reach safety. I warmly commend it.

Leonard Cheshire

Dedication

This narrative is dedicated to the many brave people in France, but for whose help during World War II it might never have been written.

The characters are real, although names have been altered in a few cases, and they were all men, women and youngsters of supreme calibre, some of whom died as a result of their efforts. They were members, sometimes leaders, of 'underground' movements. Some were simply patriotic people, coming from all walks of life. Together they played a courageous part, always with grave risks to themselves and their families.

During the journey of my fellow crewman and myself through occupied France in the winter of 1942/43, we were helped by many of these brave people, some of whom would remain unknown and unsung, because their names were never divulged to us, but undoubtedly deserve our recognition and profound gratitude. Since the war, I have many times visited the known friends who helped us, and am always greeted with warmth and affection, and treated like a returning hero. Quite the reverse is true. The heroes are those patriots, young and old, who gave so selflessly, regardless of the appalling consequences, should they have been discovered.

Apart from the evaders like myself, who keep in touch, the formation of the Royal Air Forces Escaping Society in 1945 has kept the spirit of remembrance alive, and often results in many previously unknown 'helpers', as they were termed, being brought to light, and receive the recognition they deserve. In numerous cases the Society provides financial, social and medical assistance, should they require it, and their appreciation of simply being remembered, after forty years, knows no bounds.

Never have Resistance Movements and individual patriotism

played such a large part in warfare. The debt we owe is undoubtedly priceless.

Henry Ord Robertson

Acknowledgements

The events related in my narrative took place forty-six years ago and it is mainly due to the persuasive efforts of my wife that I have finally put pen to paper at this late stage, trusting that even after over four decades there may still be an interest in the events portrayed.

In addition, many friends and relatives have asked why I have not written an account of my experiences, whilst certain organisations to whom I have given talks on behalf of the RAF Escaping Society have asked the same question.

I am therefore grateful primarily to my wife for her encouragement and again to those others who have helped to spur me on.

Grateful thanks are also due to my friends in France for helping me to retrace my steps in many parts of the country and refreshing my memory of events and incidents which might otherwise have remained forgotten.

I refer specifically to the following:

Monsieur and Madame Fernand Cherrier and various relatives who conducted me in the area of Bar-Le Duc and St Mihiel where I was shot down;

Monsieur and Madame Louis Perignon of Courouvre, who showed me the exact spot where my aircraft crashed forty-six years earlier;

Madame Monique Spiquel of Neuilly, Paris and her friends Georges Brion and Jacques Clement-Prince;

Monsieur and Madame Denivelle of Ruffec in the Charente;

Max Denivelle, their son who supplied me with wartime photographs of his parents; and

Monsieur and Madame Boulet of Verteuil near Ruffec.

Finally my thanks are due to Mrs Doreen Guest and Miss

Julia Brotherton who jointly typed the original manuscript; also to my grandniece, Helen Farrel, who was also helpful.

H.O.R.

Introduction

North-West Europe, in the post Dunkirk period, became the stage for a drama which was to have far-reaching effects, as the result of underground escape and sabotage operations. At that early stage, political complications did not enter into the sphere of operations, thus the people involved combined in what they considered to be a great human cause. It inspired people from all walks of life to risk their lives and those of their families, in this fellowship. Doctors, lawyers, businessmen and artists combined with farmers, café-owners and working class families all over occupied north-west Europe to pit their wits against the invaders, particularly against the Gestapo and the Milice, the pro-German French police.

Survivors can speak of their mistakes, dogged persistence, and enthusiasm in the face of treachery from within, as well as without. They hated tyranny, acting in the name of charity and, above all, freedom, convinced that, at the same time, they were helping the Allied cause.

After the collapse of France in 1940, the country was divided by a demarcation line. The north and west of the line was fully occupied by German troops. The southern part of the country, called the Free Zone, was administered by a puppet government under Marshal Pétain, from Vichy, and remained hostile to the Allies. It was unable to prevent large-scale escape activities after Dunkirk, when large numbers of servicemen, left marooned after the evacuation and not rounded up by the Germans, crossed the line, hoping for rescue from the Mediterranean ports of France. Many of these journeys were accomplished without papers, and sometimes still in uniform, with the help of nurses and doctors in Northern France, who passed them on to friends who, in turn, passed them on to other friends until many got through to the relative safety of the south coast.

As time wore on, such journeys became more hazardous and virtually impossible without guides, and soon French and Belgians began to organise themselves into groups, to hide and shelter them. Those who volunteered and took part in this perilous work were of every age, from the very young who acted as couriers, to the old and poor, who were able to hide and feed men on the run in defiance of the Gestapo. Eventually these groups and this form of clandestine service developed into regular, well-established and efficient escape lines from major cities in France, Holland and Belgium. Soon they began to have radio contact with military intelligence in London, who supplied money and arms, arranged the landing and evacuation of undercover agents, whose job it was to organise the resistance groups in their many activities.

In occupied France, the Gestapo and the Abwehr made the running of escape routes an extremely dangerous occupation from the beginning, and there were many casualties. In the unoccupied zone of Vichy France, where things should have been less hazardous, the security forces consisted of the hated Milice, drawn mainly from the scum of French society and French jails, and a constant menace to the Resistance Movement. There was also, however, a force of French civilian police, gendarmes, who frequently co-operated with escape workers, at great risk, and with invaluable results.

The majority of those who returned from north-west Europe were from the Allied air forces, and their return was a great morale booster to all those aircrew who were continuing to fly against Germany, whilst the feelings of the returned aircrew were a mixture of gratitude and anxiety for their helpers. The feeling of mutual gratitude and sympathy in danger continues in the work of the Royal Air Forces Escaping Society which still maintains strong contact with surviving helpers or their dependants who may be in difficulties, financial and health-wise. Even now, helpers, who have remained undis-covered for 45 years, are becoming known, and are able to provide definite proof of their activities during those momentous years.

The men who came back were divided into two categories, escapers and evaders. Numbers of the former in Western Europe were less and they were less often in the hands of secret organisations. Escapes and home runs from prison camps had less chance of success than had evasions. There were about 2,400 British and Dominion evaders from this area, and 2,700 American, few of whom would have succeeded, but for the help of the escape lines. The price paid by the underground workers for this achievement was costly. Over 500 civilians from France, Belgium and Holland were arrested, shot or died in concentration camps. A greater number died, after the war, as a result of the treatment meted out to them whilst in captivity.

The method of evasion was well defined for aircrews if they got away undetected from their aircraft, or point of landing by parachute. After making an initial contact, they usually entered a system of 'safe houses' whose owners hid them, and fed them, before sending them to a collecting point in major cities of the countries involved. Here, they would be supplied with false papers, suitable clothing, then taken by train to the frontier zone, and led by guides over the mountains into Spain. Evaders were commonly referred to as 'parcels'.

Two of the most famous lines were 'Pat' or 'O'Leary line', operating initially from Marseilles then from Toulouse, and the Comet line originating in Brussels. Many smaller groups also existed, especially in rural districts, but more often than not, their 'parcels' eventually passed through one or other of the main lines. Attempts by the Gestapo and certain traitors who served them, to infiltrate the lines, caused many breaks, necessitating men being transferred from one group to another. If the Gestapo did manage to locate a group, and discover people with British or American airmen hidden in their houses, it was the practice to 'dispose' of these so-called unimportant people, but the real leaders and organisers, if caught, were submitted to torture in an effort to reveal the wider extent of the network.

Over the escape lines, the dark wings of treachery always hovered, and of the 500 or so who died, 100 or more were betrayed by French and Belgian traitors who sold themselves to the Gestapo. Shamefully, one Englishman was known to have betrayed some of these workers.

In the following narrative, I recount my own and my companion's personal experiences, whilst in the care of the people like the ones here described. Regrettably, I live with the knowledge that many who were instrumental in our successful evasion remain unknown by name, though not in memory.

CHAPTER ONE

Target Mannheim

On Sunday 6 December 1942, the dawn slowly broke over the airfield of Linton-on-Ouse, in the same way as it was breaking over the dozens of other windswept Bomber Command airfields, thickly situated in the flat and rather featureless Vale of York.

So many were the number of Royal Air Force stations situated in this area of the North Yorkshire countryside that in many cases landing circuits almost overlapped one another, and extreme care was demanded of both aircrews and ground staff alike when aircraft were returning from operations over Europe, particularly during the early morning hours of darkness. Often the airfield beacons flashing their individual code letters were the only indication to the bomber crews that they were joining the correct airfield circuit, preparatory to landing. Apart from this potential hazard, the level nature of the countryside was ideal for the purpose for which it was being used.

Linton-on-Ouse, close to the village of Newton-on-Ouse, seven or eight miles north of the city of York, was the home of two Halifax squadrons, 76 and 78; both units of No. 4 Group Bomber Command. The former squadron had moved from Middleton-St George, in County Durham, in September and found itself sharing the airfield with 78 Squadron, commanded at that time by Wing Commander J.B. Tait. The commanding officer of 76 Squadron was Wing Commander, now Group Captain VC, Leonard Cheshire and, to quote from Andrew Boyle's excellent biography of Cheshire, *No Passing Glory*: 'In Tait he found a man after his own heart, and although lacking the easy social grace and the quick wit of Cheshire, had the similar streak of unorthodox daring and a similar flair for tactical improvisation.'

The station commander, Group Captain John Whiteley, gave his full support to the many novel ideas produced by his two squadron commanders.

Cheshire had a unique and attractive personality and soon won the confidence of every officer and all other ranks on the station. He was only 25, the youngest wing commander in the service, I believe, but at the same time very mature in his outlook. In order to get his way over some idea and in support of an argument, he could be so politely determined that he rarely failed in his efforts to convince his opposers.

To his advice, and rather uncanny foresight, I'm convinced I owe the initial part of my successful evasion. For instance, he used to give informal lectures on the problems which could be faced by the crews of aircraft who found themselves shot down in enemy territory, or as a result of severe damage to the aircraft, had to bail out over hostile terrain.

'I know,' he used to say, 'it is your duty, wherever possible to evade capture, or escape after capture but, in addition, it will be in your own interests to get away without delay from the scene, because the time will surely come when the Germans resort to shooting prisoners of war on any pretext.'

How true this prophecy turned out to be when 50 escaping officers from Stalagluft III were shot, all in one batch, on the justification that they were attempting to escape.

We all listened attentively to his advice, and although convinced that he was probably right, thought, it might happen to some, but it won't happen to me.

When the time came, and it *did* happen to me, one of my first thoughts was to remember his advice, and, automatically putting it into practice initially, it proved to be a vital factor in my ultimate salvation.

I had been trained as a wireless operator, and together with Pilot Officer Bill Hillier, the skipper, and Sergeant H.B. Canter, navigator, had passed through Operational Training School at Kinloss, as a crew; were posted to Middleton St George, and ultimately to Linton-on-Ouse when the whole squadron moved in September. Here we were crewed up with the other four crew members necessary to form the seven-man crew of a Halifax bomber, namely Sergeant McDonald, a Canadian, as bomb aimer. Sergeant 'Johnny' Parkin, flight engineer, Sergeant Jack Theckston, mid-upper gunner, and

Sergeant E.A. Smith, rear gunner. I knew little of the civilian occupations of my crew, but I believe Hillier, who came from Brighton, was a civil servant, Canter was a chemist, whilst my occupation was a clerical one with the LNER Company, and from the outset, as a crew, we got on very well with one another.

Before actually meeting up with Bill Hillier, Canter and I had been flying together with various pilots, in Anson and Whitley aircraft at No. 19 OTU Kinloss and it was with this unit that we both had the experience of bailing out during a night cross-country exercise in an Anson. In gradually worsening weather conditions, the radio packed up, we got hopelessly lost in and above heavy cloud whose base level was well below mountain summits in Scotland, eventually ran out of petrol and were forced to abandon the aircraft over mountainous country, inland from Aberdeen. For Canter and myself, this was to be something of a practice jump, for what was to happen at a later date, in vastly different circumstances of course.

Soon after this episode, Hillier became our permanent skipper and the three of us knew one another quite well when we subsequently arrived at Linton. Together with McDonald, Parkin, Theckston and Smith we became quite a capable team during the three months we operated together.

The months of October and November saw us complete nine operations, over Flensburg, Krefeld, Aachen, Osnabrück, Kiel, Cologne, Genoa and two trips to Turin. The trip to Kiel resulted in the aircraft being so severely damaged by flak over the target that it was written off after returning on three engines. It was only due to Hillier's skill, after being coned by searchlights and losing a starboard engine, that we got back at all.

The last trip we had done was to Turin on 28 November which we reckoned had been a piece of cake with very little opposition over the target, the greatest danger being from night fighters during the long flight across France, the Alps and Northern Italy. So we reckoned on the morning of 6 December that our period of operational inactivity could hardly last much longer.

All NCO aircrews were billeted at this period in Beningboro Hall, home of Lady Chesterfield, which had been taken over by the War Office. Officers were accommodated in the officers' mess on the station. After breakfast we cycled the two or three miles to the airfield, where we immediately got the distinct impression that our reckoning had been correct. The place was a hive of activity. Across the runways and round the perimeter track where the Halifaxes were dispersed on the hard-standings, came the roar of engines being run up, whilst here and there, could be seen bomb trains trundling out, under the bright winter's sunshine, over the early morning frosted grass, heading for the dispersal pads.

No doubt about it, all this activity pointed in one direction only. We would be 'on' tonight. Any thoughts of another binge that evening in York took a sharp nosedive.

Life on a Bomber Command station, was, to say the least, a peculiar state of existence, almost like living in two worlds. One night a crew could be sitting in a York cinema watching *Gone with the Wind*, as we were one evening, or perhaps having a heavy drinking session in Betty's Bar and learning all the up-to-date news concerning the well-being, or otherwise, of friends or acquaintances serving in other squadrons of the Group.

'Roger just made it last night. Last trip of his tour! Staggered into Marston Moor on two engines, no undercart, mid-upper dead and rear gunner had bailed out in mistake.'

'Roger Murdoch, you mean?'

'Yes, Roger the dodger. One other kite didn't get back but I don't know whose it was.'

'Hell! Where had they been?'

'Frankfurt.'

'Chris has been posted. Finished his tour last week and gone to Transport Command, at his own request.'

'Lucky bloke. Probably shuttling VIPs to and fro instead of laying eggs in Germany.'

So it would go on.

The following night, the same crew would be bucking about over some German city in a hell of searchlights, heavy and light flak, the area below looking like something out of Dante's Inferno, punctuated by the flickering flashes of gunfire, the heavier flashes of bursting bombs and overall, the red glow through the smoke from burning buildings. Occasionally a vivid explosion in the sky would signal a direct hit on some poor devil, or a four-engined aircraft would stand on one wing tip, then gently spiral down with flames pouring back from one or more engines. Sometimes parachutes would blossom out, sometimes not a far cry from a comfortable cinema seat in York.

Last night we had enjoyed a convivial evening across the river, drinking, chatting and playing dominoes or darts with the locals in the Alice Hawthorn pub, by the village green in Nun Monkton. By the looks of things, tonight would not be so congenial.

Bill Hillier, as a commissioned officer, was billeted in the officers' quarters on the main station, and we would no doubt find him, in due course, in the area of the flight officers or crew rooms adjacent to the hangars. We made for squadron headquarters, and, sure enough, the order of battle was already pinned up on the notice board, showing which crews would be 'on' this evening, the aircraft allotted to them and time of briefing. Our last two trips – both to Turin – had been in 'P' for Popsie, and the same aircraft had been allotted to us once again. The target, of course, was unknown as yet, and would not be divulged until the main briefing. Navigators and pilots, however, were usually aware of the target before the rest of their crew since they needed somewhat more time for preparation of the flight plan in the navigation section.

We eventually located Bill, who had already been out to dispersal and had some talk with the aircraft ground crew, who were now well into their daily inspections. The armourers would probably be there now checking the long chains of ammunition for free movement in the ammunition tracks leading from the turrets along the inside fuselage to the carrier boxes, then feeding the belts into the gun breeches.

On completion of their tasks, the aircraft would be ready for each of us to begin our own individual checks, satisfy ourselves that all was well and wring out any wrinkles on an air test, before lunch, and report our findings to the ground crew. Bill and 'Eddy' (Canter, the navigator, inevitably was nicknamed after the film personality) then made off to the navigation section, where, as I have already said, they would learn the target and commence the necessary flight-planning.

There was little we could do in the meantime, before Hillier and Canter came back to do an air test, and we went to the NAAFI, sat down to 'tea and wads' and discussed the probabilities of the target, somewhat excited perhaps, yet inwardly a little fearful; keen but uncertain, wanting to get on with it, but hoping all the while for a 'scrub'.

It was a common belief among air crews that the first five or six operations were the most dangerous, and if you had successfully completed that quota you were over the first hurdle, considered to be old hands and could hopefully consider possible survival during the next twenty-four or -five trips and so complete a tour. I suppose this kind of belief tended to buck up one's ego for a while, but it didn't always prove to be anything of a certainty. We had, up to now, completed nine, so perhaps now as 'old hands' there was hope.

We went out to the dispersal to meet Bill and Eddy for the air test, and stood around chatting to the ground crew for a few minutes until they arrived. The skipper walked round the Halifax checking externally the air frame, flaps, ailerons, trimming tabs, rudders, tyres and undercart, bomb doors, elevators and pilot head, then climbed in and went up front to the cockpit. We followed him in, going to our respective positions for individual checks, gunners to check ammunition, cocking the guns once or twice to ensure no jamming in the chutes, testing rotation of their turrets, hydraulically and manually, depression and elevation of the Brownings and the electrically luminated ring sights. As wireless operator I checked over the 1154 and 1155 transmitter and receiver, intercom, trailing ariel for easy winding, the loop ariel, the IFF equipment (identification friend or foe), the morse key and click stop calibrations. The engineer did his engine panel check and the skipper his cockpit check, whilst the bomb aimer tested switches, bomb selectors and bomb sight.

Bill had a quick word or two with the flight sergeant in charge of the ground crew before starting engines and we took off for the short test flight to ascertain that everything was satisfactory when airborne. We returned after twenty minutes or so to dispersal, where the ground crew were anxiously waiting, hoping that no serious snaggs had cropped up and the gremlins had not been busy.

Everything was OK and we made off to our respective messes for lunch, leaving the armourers who were standing by waiting to bomb-up, sitting on their long caterpillar trailers loaded with the necessary type of bombs for our, as yet, unknown target.

It was often possible to glean an idea of the proximity and type of target from the size and composition of the bomb load, high explosive, armour piercing and incendiary, or a combination perhaps of HE and incendiary. In this instance, we noted the accent was mainly on 1000 lb HEs and a proportion of incendiaries, which indicated a flight of short or medium duration, with little penetration into Germany proper, thus giving us transient reassurance.

After lunch crew members began converging on the briefing room in little groups and ones and twos, and by 2 p.m. we were all gathered together on the uncomfortable fold-up chairs, facing the small dais at the far end, apprehensively awaiting the removal of the curtain which concealed the large target map which covered the greater part of the wall, behind the dais. There was a scraping of chair legs over the bare floor as we hurriedly scrambled to our feet on the entrance of the station commander, followed by his squadron commanders and the various briefing officers. They all took their places on the dais, the station commander signalled removal of the curtain, and all was revealed. A red tape stretched from Linton to a point near Eastbourne, across the English channel, zigzagged across France, avoiding wherever possible those large red blotches on the map which signified concentrated flak areas or known night-fighter control beacons, and terminated at Mannheim.

There was a subdued buzz of conversation, a few rather more audible comments, a few sighs, and generally, an atmosphere of relief that it was not to be a dance of death in 'Happy Valley' – the Ruhr – or alternatively, a long dangerous flight to Magdeburg, Frankfurt or Berlin.

The met officer was the first to speak and display large complicated weather charts showing present conditions over the UK and Europe, the expected conditions during the flight and over the target, and finally weather expectations over the airfield for the returning bombers. Most of the technical detail was lost on many crews who were forced to fall back on his general description at the end, which we hoped indicated reasonable conditions. The weather over northern Europe during the past month of November had been exceedingly bad. Time after time crews returned frustrated by sudden changes in the forecast winds, while near unbroken cloud seemed to be a nightly feature over Germany at the time. Hence the general pattern of successes against the Italian targets. Perhaps this was to be the beginning of a change in the weather pattern.

Then came the station intelligence officer. He talked briefly about the target area, its military importance and contribution to Germany's war effort, the aiming points and immediate city defences. He pointed out the known position of flak batteries and fighter-controlled areas en route, and strength of flak and searchlight opposition expected over the target.

A few brief words were then said by the signals and navigation officers regarding radio frequencies and DF stations available for obtaining loop bearings and fixes. Radio silence was of course to be maintained throughout except in extreme emergency. Checks of the forecast winds was emphasised by the taking of loop bearings, drift sights and astro procedure and by visual pinpoints, if weather conditions and cloud formation permitted.

Finally the CO gave us recommended bombing heights, the total number of aircraft over the target, with a warning to maintain a sharp lookout to avoid collisions: order and times of take-off at one minute intervals. He briefly glanced round at the map behind him and turned back to face us.

'Good luck,' he said.

'Hit it hard,' and he stepped down from the dais, whilst we again hurriedly scrambled to our feet as he departed.

We filed out of the room and dispersed in groups to our various sections and locker rooms to sort out and collect our equipment, maps, charts, compasses and dividers, rulers, pencils, rubber, computers, sextants, astro-tables, watches, protractors, log books, Very cartridges, radio codes on destructible edible rice paper, pocket escape kits, flying rations and coffee flasks.

Pre-operational tea was at 1530 hours and take-off time started at 1645 hours. We arrived in the crew room after the meal at about 1600 hours, having collected our parachutes from the section on the way, and found the usual babble of noise and disarray. The air was filled with spontaneous chatter, convulsive mirth and ribald remarks, with periodic loud-voiced interruptions when someone couldn't find something or other and accused somebody else of 'half-inching' his gloves, scarf or other piece of personal equipment. Everywhere was a jumble of parachutes, boots, helmets and blokes struggling into unwieldy flying clothing, particularly the gunners. Here and there the atmosphere was obviously forced, more particularly among crews who were making their first trip, mentally trying to discount the many rumours and tales of alarming incidents and 'shaky do's' on the way to, and over, the target, whilst at the same time trying to remember all they had been taught at OTU in preparation for the baptism of action, and contemplating what it actually would be like.

Personally, I never wore full flying gear, finding it too cumbersome in the confined space of the wireless compartment. Anyway, that position, together with that of the navigator, tended to get very warm even at extreme heights, being very close to the main heater outlets. I therefore concentrated on warm underwear, sleeved vest and Long Johns, roll-necked, thigh-length white sweater, flying boots and silk-inner gloves. The gunners all wore full gear, of course, even to the extent of electrically heated outer suits, to combat the intense cold which could be experienced, particularly in the nearly isolated rear turret when flying at twelve thousand feet and over.

Suddenly a voice yelled: 'Everybody out, transport's here,' and the crew buses are rolling to a halt outside the locker room. We step outside and prepare to board. It was not so bad while one was kept busy in the crew room collecting equipment and donning flying kit, joking and chattering to friends and neighbours, but once inside the bus or truck, the churning would start in one's stomach. The feeling was somewhat akin to sitting in a waiting room, awaiting your turn in the dentist's chair. The eagerness to be away and airborne is diminished by the awareness that everyone who had scrambled noisily aboard the transport this evening would not necessarily share the thankful journey back in a few hours' time. Of course, each one muses, I'll be all right; everyone thinks that of himself. One or two, or more, of the other blokes might be unlucky, but I'll be OK. The 'other blokes' are, of course, thinking exactly the same about you.

And so we bumped round the peri-track till the vast shadow of a Halifax appeared out of the gloom, sitting like a monstrous prehistoric bird, on its dispersal. The bus stopped with a jerk.

' "Q" for Queenie,' somebody called from the driver's cab; 'Anybody for "Q"?'

'Yes, yes, hang on a minute. Don't be in such a goddamned hurry,' and seven blokes scrambled out.

'See you in the morning, laddie.'

'OK, Mac. All the best.'

Off we go again.

' "N" for nuts anyone?'

'Yeah, OK.'

'Out you go then. Cheerio, Taffy,' and another seven bodies descend.

And so it went on, until, arriving at 'P' for Popsie, we in turn scrambled out. Wing Commander Cheshire, our squadron CO, appeared out of the late afternoon dimness and wished us a good trip and good luck. He did this with every crew as far as he could, it being his custom to follow the crew transports around in his own car, or sometimes on a bicycle, to the various dispersals and wish each crew good luck. Afterwards he would return to the flight or the airfield control tower to watch take-off.

The huge four-engined Halifaxes at their dispersals take on an ever more menacing and darkened shape in the fast gathering gloom of a December afternoon. It is a time when all that has to be done before an operation, has been done. The bombing up and fuelling is finished, internal individual checks have been completed and the F 700s have been signed by the skippers. Our pre-operational tasks are complete, the future depends upon God, the weather, our own skill, a helluva lot of luck, and the hope that we can avoid the worst that the Hun can send against us.

The prelude would last for another twenty minutes, the first aircraft being due off at 1645 hours. During that twenty minutes the quiet of the evening vibrated with the sound of mighty Merlin engines starting up all round the perimeter of the airfield. The WAAF drivers had departed back to the section with their empty buses and trucks, and the usual little knot of people began to gather at the start of the runway to wave us off. The starter battery was in place under the wing of 'Popsie' with the ground crew standing by.

We climbed into the aircraft, took up our respective positions and plugged into the intercom sockets. After strapping himself into his seat, Bill slid open his side window and shouted down to the ground-crew NCO.

'OK for starting up?'

'OK, sir.'

'Stand clear, contact port outer.'

'Contact!'

The engine turned over once, twice, then belched a mass of black smoke and roared into life. Bill throttled back.

'Contact, port inner!'

'Contact!'

And number two engine roared into life. Similarly both starboard engines were started, the starter trolley disconnected and pulled away. There followed a short period of settling down, juggling the throttles and synchronising and a general testing of intercom. One by one the OKs came round from gunners, navigator, engineer, bomb aimer and myself.

All four engines were run up to full revs by Bill, with the assistance of the engineer, and petrol cocks, magnetos, pitch controls and boost were re-checked on each engine. Bomb doors, flaps and rudders were operated; the compass and gyro set.

We waited for time to taxi.

CHAPTER TWO

Death of a Halifax

'Stand by to taxi!'

The chocks were waved away and pulled clear by the ground crew; brakes were released and we moved out to join the slowly moving queue of Halifaxes waddling round the perimeter track towards the runway threshold. To the little group of people outside waiting to cheer us off, the cacophony of noise from up to 100 Merlin engines, must have been deafening to the ear, and this was punctuated by hisses and squeals from protesting brakes, as each aircraft was checked by its pilot, to prevent running into the bomber ahead. The procession was headed by 'D' Dog, followed by 'S' Sugar, 'M' Mother, 'Q' Queenie, 'N' Nuts, 'R' Robert then our 'P' Popsie – seventh in order of take-off.

One by one the preceding six bombers reached the threshold, and took off on receipt of a green light from runway control caravan. We reached the intersection, turned on to the runway and halted, engines idling. The green light flashed from the caravan, the throttles were advanced to full power, the aircraft straining on the brakes, which were suddenly released, and we were on our way, tearing down the runway, pilot and engineer co-operating together with throttles, flaps and undercarriage. Throttles go through the gate and are held by the engineer, the ASI registered 120, and Bill eased back on the control column and we were airborne; the wings distinctly shudder and flutter under the cushion of air. The nose dipped a degree or so, as the undercart comes up, tucks into each inner engine nacelle with a slight clunk and is recorded on the cockpit panel by red lights winking out. Above 500 feet the nose dips again as the flaps are retracted in five degree snatches and the pilot trims to compensate.

With revs at 2850, the Halifax settles into a steady climb at

160 mph to reach recommended height, and the operation has begun. All doubts, fears and butterflies magically disappear as we concentrate on our individual tasks. Canter called out the first course, Bill checked it back verbally and set it on the compass. I checked and set up the pre-set radio frequencies on receiver and transmitter, switched on the IFF, reeled out the trailing area and reported OK to the skipper. As previously stated, radio silence was essential, since the enemy could pick up radio transmission and deduce that an operation was afoot and sometimes glean a rough idea of the proposed target area. It was necessary to 'listen out' on base frequency at certain times in case of any change of orders, or a recall. In addition, loop bearings could be taken in perfect safety, passed to the navigator, and, when plotted enable him to fix our position, and so check the accuracy of our track and the forecast winds. The engineer concentrated on his panels and passed any necessary information to the skipper.

'Permission to test guns, skipper?' called Smithy from the rear turret.

'OK, go ahead, quickly, and keep your eyes peeled.'

There then came the brief clatter of the four Brownings and silence.

From the mid-upper:

'OK to test also,' from Jack Theckston.

'Yeah, go ahead.'

The gunners would then settle down swinging their turrets and searching the sky methodically for other aircraft, friendly or otherwise.

From the rear turret suddenly came the unharmonic strains of 'You are my sunshine, my only sunshine,' Smithy's favourite song.

'For God's sake Smithy, shut off your microphone,' shouted Bill angrily.

Silence, then: 'OK, skip, sorry,' and there was a click as the mike was switched off.

On frequent occasions a crew member inadvertently left his microphone switched on, and when the oxygen mask, which also contained the mike was hanging loose, all background noises were audible through the intercom system and could seriously interfere with any really necessary conversation between other crew members. Hence the pilot's temporary annoyance and a reminder to all of us to ensure 'microphones off'.

We had now reached cruising height and 'Popsie' pressed on, smoothly and steadily into the swiftly growing darkness. There was no moon, very little cloud and the stars were beginning to become visible. Now and again the vague dark shape of another Halifax, Lancaster or Wellington would appear through the gloom, and sometimes our aircraft would buck suddenly as we were caught in the slipstream of an aircraft ahead of us.

As it continued to become darker, we then began to feel more and more alone and isolated. Hillier would constantly call to the two gunners and the bomb aimer, who was now occupying the second pilot's seat, to keep a sharp look-out for accompanying aircraft.

Canter's voice came over the intercom.

'New course, skipper.'

'What?' from Bill.

'Time to alter course, skipper. We're approaching rendezvous point.'

We were to rendezvous with other squadrons of the bomber force of Beachy Head, where we would alter course, crossing the enemy coast over Flanders to steer south of Antwerp towards Aachen.

'OK, navigator, altering course to – what was it again, 090°?'

'Correct skipper, 090° magnetic, and please keep your air speed constant.'

I heard Bill breath hard into his mike and mutter:

'OK!'

Fluctuating air speed, even when correctly on course, can affect precise navigation, and no pilot ever relishes being reminded of the fact.

We were now heading out to sea, and very soon approaching the hostile Belgian coastline.

Drawing aside the black-out curtain of the window in the port side of the wireless compartment, I saw one or two desultory bursts of flak to the north, but too far away to be of any menace, and probably directed at a diversionary mine-laying operation. I turned back to the radio and listened out at the set time, having to concentrate very hard in an effort to hear, through the very heavy atmospheric interference and static, any vital transmission from the base that might have any direct effect on our object, but received nothing. I tuned in to some dance music coming over on the BBC frequency, when Canter suddenly called me and asked for a couple of bearings. I obliged, and shortly he called out a slight alteration in course. We must have drifted a little off track.

We carried on uneventfully for a while, then:

'Skipper!'

'Yes!'

'Time to alter course again. Steer 140° magnetic. This is the last leg before target approach.'

'Ok, nav, 140 it is. Hallo, gunners, keep a sharp lookout. There's a fighter control zone just south of our track.'

Both gunners acknowledged.

Very soon we were dead on track, the defences of Mannheim would appear ahead. All being well, another half hour would see us releasing our cargo and making our way back home, or so I thought. How wrong I was to be.

For two members of the crew this was to be a very short operation, the outward trip of which would not be completed and there would be no return. For three others, it was destined to be a much longer affair, three years longer in fact, their return being interrupted by a three year stint 'in the cage' as POWs. For the remaining two, which included me, the operation which should have lasted for four or five hours, would be extended to a duration of nearly five months, during which time a precarious, sometimes exciting, often boring and uneventful, but nevertheless dangerous existence in occupied territory would be experienced.

We flew steadily south-eastwards on the new course, Canter hunched over his charts and navigational equipment, whilst I experimented with the radio key, on a specially provided frequency, which, in conjunction with the IFF system, was supposed to interfere and jam the German Freya, a ground-controlled radar system designed to detect the bomber force and vector night fighters into the stream. True, I could discern, through severe static a jumble of plain language, obviously German, but I had no means of knowing whether my jamming device was effective. In view of what was to happen next, I haven't the least hesitation in saying that it definitely wasn't.

The silence in the aircraft was suddenly and rudely shattered by a loud sustained burst of heavy cannon or machine gun fire. The bomber shuddered violently, and I experienced the distinct and extraordinary sensation that we had stopped, in mid-air, and the previous silence became almost oppressive.

Over the intercom came the voice of the skipper:

'Christ! what the hell was that? Oh, my God.'

I shot a glance around the compartment and everything appeared to be normal, except for the navigator who was looking directly at me with a puzzled and rather questioning expression on his face.

'Engineer here, skip. Port outer engine on fire. Jesus, the inner looks to be starting as well.'

'Bloody hell!'

I glanced through my little port window and saw flames from both port engines streaming back over the wing surface.

A second or two more and, the intercom spluttered again.

'I've tried the fire extinguishers but they aren't having any effect. Diving!'

Bill put the Halifax into a steep stomach-churning dive in an effort to douse the fire, but with no success. He levelled out and called:

'It looks as though we'll have to abandon, chaps.'

The gun fire had come from directly below us, neither of the two gunners having seen our attackers. In the light of future knowledge this was perfectly understandable, the gunners being entirely blameless. The technique used by the fighter was completely new, and in the future, was to prove to be extremely successful from the German point of view. Generally fighter attacks, by day or night, came from direct astern, or from either beam of the bomber, and so long as the gunners were on their toes, warning could be given to the pilot, who would take the necessary evasive action and often escape.

This new type of attack involved the night-fighter pilot being directed by ground control, on to a specified target, approach from well in the rear and below the bomber's height until directly underneath the victim's belly and unseen by either gunner, then to open fire with upward firing cannons, aiming directly at its engines. The aircraft used for this type of attack were modified Me110s or Junkers 88s carrying a crew of three, pilot, radar operator and gunner, and using their upward-firing guns, 'Schräge Musik' as they were called, were extremely successful in the interception and destruction of many unsuspecting Allied machines.

I learned later that we were a victim of this type of attack and the fighter concerned was based at St Dizier, a former French airfield. My mid-upper gunner, Sergeant Theckston, actually met and talked to the German pilot who shot us down, whilst waiting at Bar-le-Duc for transportation to a POW camp.

The whole of the front interior of the Halifax was now bathed in bright orange light coming from the blazing port engines, but Bill was still in control and keeping her on even keel.

I switched over to distress frequency on the transmitter, tapped out our call sign and clamped down the morse key, in the hope that some ground operator might pick up the signal and learn a little of our predicament and position, not that he could do anything practical about the situation. Then I chewed up the destructible radio codes, swallowed them and then destroyed the secret IFF equipment. I glimpsed Canter kick up his folding table and yank up the forward escape hatch in the floor adjacent to his seat, whilst the bomb-aimer was climbing down from the second pilot's seat, grabbing his parachute from its storage as he did so.

Again, over the intercom:

'OK, chaps, prepare to bale out! – Jump! Jump!'

At this moment the voice of the rear gunner came over the intercom enquiring:

'Did you say jump, skip?'

I remember thinking to myself, what a helluva time to hold a debate, and ask silly questions.

The inrush of air from the open escape hatch blew charts, maps, codes and writing materials all over the cabin, and through the shower of paper I saw Canter snap on his parachute, dangle his legs through the hatch and suddenly disappear. The bomb-aimer followed immediately and I found my parachute and began clipping it to my harness.

Johny Parkin, the engineer, was next to go, and, sitting on the edge of the escape hatch, his legs dangling in the slipstream, his face wore a really comical expression of combined disbelief, ruefulness, disgust and dismay, as he gave me a brief wave and was gone.

I called to Bill over the intercom: 'Wireless operator baling out skipper,' pulled off my flying helmet, scrambled to the hatch, and dropped into the void.

I don't remember whether I counted the requisite number of seconds before pulling the ripcord D-ring, but I must have been clear of the doomed Halifax because of a sudden jerk arrested my fall and informed me the chute had opened. Glancing upwards the canopy was fully opened, and above that I glimpsed poor old 'P' Popsie, fire pouring from both port engines and wing trailing edge, still flying straight and level, heading away into the darkness.

Only seconds had elapsed since the burst of the night fighter's guns, the order to 'bale out' and this moment when I was gently penduling down in the darkness, only the sound of the wind rustling through the rigging cords of the parachute as music to my ears. There hadn't been much time for rational thinking during those few seconds, and my thoughts, as I remember them now, were a very mixed bunch.

The first, I remember most vividly. It was the realisation that I wasn't likely to be returning to the sergeants' mess that night for bacon and eggs. That thought predominated over all others, which were of a much more disturbing and important nature, when I did get round to considering them. Once I had accepted that, the unreality of the situation flicked through my mind. This kind of thing had happened many times before, but to chaps whom I had known on the squadron; it wasn't likely to happen to me. But it had – there wasn't the slightest doubt about it.

The ludicrousness of my predicament struck me. Here I was, suspended by the silken cords and canopy of a parachute, in the darkness of the evening sky, somewhere over Europe, gently floating down to – where? What would my people at home think if they could see me now? Would they think the same, that it couldn't happen to Harry, and maybe see the comical side of the situation?

Then suddenly and soberly, the utter reality of the situation dawned upon me. It wasn't comical, it wasn't fantasy, it was for real.

Where was the night fighter? Was he still mooching about looking for me, to finish the business with another burst of fire? Would he accidentally fly into me or the parachute in the darkness.

No. He would be far above me now, probably following the blazing Halifax and making sure of his 'kill'.

I suddenly became aware that I was still hanging on to the metal D-ring of the parachute. During my period of operational training at Kinloss, I remember being told that if, for any reason, we had to use our parachutes and we didn't return the ring to the parachute section, it would cost us 2/6d (12½p), so when we did have to bale out over Scotland, as I have already mentioned, we were all careful to return our D-rings to the section when we got back to Kinloss. It occurred to me now that the chances of returning a halfcrown's worth of equipment to the parachute section, after completion of this venture, were definitely non-existent, so I dropped it.

As I looked down and saw it disappear, two more thoughts entered my mind. Where was I? What kind of a reception, if any, awaited me when I landed? Shortly before the attack, we had altered course on to the final leg of our approach towards the target, and therefore we would be flying very close to the frontier area between France and Germany. so where was I going to land, east or west of the border? I must be getting close to the ground by now, I thought, but couldn't see a thing through the darkness below me, so I kept as loose-limbed as possible to ensure an accident-free landing.

Quite suddenly, I hit the ground, fairly reasonably I thought, on what seemed to be a fairly hard surface, rolled over once, whilst the silk canopy gently collapsed around me. It was deadly quiet, I could almost feel the silence, and it was very, very dark. The only noise I became aware of was the drone of engines high above me, as the remainder of the bomber stream carried on to the east.

Immediately the thought again came to me, more urgently now I was down, where was I? France or Germany? No matter I decided, whether France or Germany, the enemy would be around somewhere, and, for sure, someone would have heard the gunfire and seen the aircraft start to burn and maybe see the parachutes come out, open and fall, and institute an immediate search for the aircraft and crew: dead or alive.

Hitting the quick release button, the parachute harness fell away from me and I scrambled to my feet to take stock of my surroundings. I had landed slap bang on a fairly hard-surfaced, light-coloured, narrow road, flanked on both sides by tall trees, and looking up, I could just discern the lighter colour of the evening sky. I was obviously in a wood, a copse or possibly a forest. Still there was silence except for the now fainter noise of the bomber stream, in the distance. There was no unwelcome reception committee – yet!

Then Leonard Cheshire's words came to me:

'It's your duty to escape or evade, but also in your own interest, make every effort to get away, escape or avoid capture.'

I moved quickly, gathered up the silk parachute canopy and the harness, pushed them securely out of sight into the thick undergrowth and trees bordering the road, and moved in among the trees. The other chaps must be around somewhere near, I thought, and moving carefully through the darkness, I called in a subdued low tone voice:

'Eddy?'

'Johnny?'

'Jack?'

'Skipper?'

No answer, not a sound. It was quite eerie!

I kept on moving through the trees parallel to the narrow road and came into a kind of clearing in the trees, which stretched to the road. Here, there were piled a number of freshly cut tree trunks, arranged in small piles, one on top of the other. I walked around in and out of the piles calling again quietly, but once more, with no reply. I was definitely on my own and decided to put Cheshire's advice into operation without further delay. I extracted from the emergency escape kit, the little compass, discovered which was roughly direction west, where home and beauty lay, and found that the narrow road through the trees ran roughly east to west. A check on personal possessions revealed that in spite of the haste in abandoning the aircraft, I had managed to stuff two small bars of chocolate and a smaller packet of biscuits in my battledress blouse, whilst a cigarette case which I always carried contained three cigarettes. I was also a pipe smoker, and as such was issued with a special escape pipe which could be smoked normally, but also had a small compass concealed in the stem. Unfortunately, I hadn't any tobacco.

I checked the emergency escape kit, a flat plastic box, which fitted neatly into the front pocket of my uniform trousers. As well as the tiny compass, it contained a small slab of highly concentrated chocolate, Horlicks tablets, concentrated vitamin tablets, booster energy tablets, water purifying tablets and fold-up rubber water carrying bottle, a large handkerchief-size silk map of France and Belgium, antiseptic ointment and sunburn cream, a quantity of French and Belgian currency, and finally a thin two inch long glass capsule labelled '20 hypodermic tablets No.35, Hyoscine Hydrobrom gr 1/100, manufactured by Boots'. This was also labelled 'poison' in red print. I never discovered the reason for the last mentioned item.

I turned my battledress blouse inside out as a feeble measure of disguising my uniform, tucked the legs of my flying boots under my trousers and started walking. My watch showed the time as 1955 hours, only 25 minutes since the night fighter had attacked. In that short time, the future had become undeniably non-predictable.

I hadn't been walking for much longer than twenty minutes or so when I heard someone whistling, not calling, but whistling a tune. I stopped, and sure enough I heard footsteps approaching along the path. I dived into the dense undergrowth bordering the road, rolled into a shallow ditch and lay flat. The footsteps and the whistling got louder as the person approached, and I sensed whoever it was passing along the path. I waited a minute or two, hearing the footsteps retreating and climbed out of the ditch and carried on walking. Fortunately the ditch had been quite dry, if a little muddy – but gosh, jolly cold. It was of course December, I remembered, and owing to all the previous excitement, I had never felt cold until now. Minor paths deviated from this main road through the forest at frequent intervals. I investigated one or two, occasionally again making subdued calls, in the hope that other of the crew members may be in the vicinity, but I heard nothing and kept going along the main path which wound and curved through the trees, changing direction frequently and failing to give any indication of breaking out into open country.

I was still theorising and trying to weigh up which side of the border I might be, but certainly I wasn't getting any help from my immediate surroundings. After all, I argued, a forest or wood in France is hardly any different from one in Germany, and until I got clear of the trees and into open country, I was unlikely to find out where I was. The escape map at present, would only be useful as a handkerchief.

Then I heard another sound, the sound of an engine, in the distance at the moment, but quickly getting louder as it approached; this time it was behind me, travelling in the same direction as myself. Whoever the previous pedestrian had been it was more than likely it had been a civilian, French or German, depending on which country I was in, perhaps returning from work in the forest; but motor transport, I reckoned, whether in Germany or France, might mean military transport, of one sort or another. So once more I dived into the bordering undergrowth and the darkness of the trees and hugged the ground. The sound of engines gradually increased and soon they were passing the spot where I was concealed. Although I dared not attempt to raise my head to identify what it was, I concluded that it was a car, lorry or van accompanied by two following motorcycles, and they passed unsuspectingly by at a steady speed, and soon the sound of the engines was dying away in the distance. Surely this couldn't already be the start of an organised search, so soon after the aircraft was seen to be on fire and had probably by now crashed? I hoped not!

Climbing out of the ditch and undergrowth, I continued walking, ready to make a hasty exit off the road again should I hear anyone or anything else approach, and still thinking and wondering what had happened to the rest of the crew. I knew Canter, Parkin and McDonald had baled out OK; I'd seen them go before I made my own exit and hoped they had made safe landings. I assumed Theckston and Smithy, the two gunners, would get out, one by the rear door, the other from the gun turret, although I hadn't heard either of them over the intercom. That left Bill Hillier, the skipper, and he was still in control and uninjured when I jumped. There was no reason to suppose that he had any difficulty leaving the aircraft. There was no strong wind to cause drifting of the parachutes, so they couldn't be too far away, probably all somewhere in this forest.

On two more occasions I was forced to avoid passers-by, one of whom I'm certain was riding a bicycle. After another short spell of walking and still shut in by trees on either side, I decided to have another go along one or two of the subsidiary paths leading off the road, still with the hope of meeting one or more of the chaps. As a result I more or less got lost, or rather more correctly, realised that I was probably going round in circles; I certainly wasn't having much success getting out of this damned forest. It must stretch for miles I thought, and I was somewhat fed up and frustrated. I longed for a cigarette, but realised that it would be unwise at the moment and, anyway, I hadn't any matches.

Then, suddenly, I found myself in a very small clearing where three paths met – one better surfaced than the others and wider – and I was sure after my haphazard wanderings among the trees, I was probably rejoining the original path on which I had landed and commenced my journey. I was feeling a bit peckish and my watch indicated the time as just after 10 pm. I sat down with my back against the base of a young tree, opened my packet of biscuits and nibbled one, broke off a square of chocolate and carefully made it last as long as possible.

As I ate, the realisation of loneliness became rather unnerving. All around the conifers of the little clearing and junction of footpaths was the sombre darkness of the tall trees and a profound silence. Oh for the companionship of one or more of the crew, to argue with, share confidence and with whom to discuss some kind of plan. What kind of a chance did I stand, stuck in this extensive forest, in enemy territory and liable to be shot on sight, or at best, captured when discovered, and finish up in 'the bag'? Wouldn't it be easier to give myself up when the opportunity arose and become a live prisoner, rather than a dead evader? Then again I remembered Cheshire's advice: 'It's part of the job to escape. It's a laid down duty, but what is more, consider self-preservation and the possible consequences of captivity.'

I had time to consider my position. I thought that this was decidedly the worst I had ever been in during my young life. Here I was, stuck in a forest of unknown dimensions, in a foreign country, with many miles of enemy-occupied territory between myself and safety, and all I had were the clothes I stood up in, an escape pack and my only weapon, a scout's sheath knife, which I had always carried. Enough to depress the most optimistic of persons one would have thought, yet, strangely enough, I wasn't really depressed. Frustrated at not being able to get out of this forest, curious and perturbed about the fate of my comrades, anxious about my whereabouts, and the threat of being pursued, but not depressed.

Of course, it was most unlikely that any co-ordinated search was being made so soon, unless the bomber had crashed in the vicinity of an area of German troop concentration, or maybe an airfield. Anyway, it was probable that until our parachutes and harnesses were found, people, friend or foe alike, would assume we had perished in the burning aircraft, and until the wreckage was investigated, the hunt would be postponed. Some of the local populace could have seen the aircraft go down, or at least, were aware of where the bomber lay burning, and may be on the lookout for survivors, particularly if the crash was in France.

It is said that to a dying or drowning man, all the events of his past life pass swiftly through his mind. Whether this is true or false, I know not, but I was not dying and had no intention of doing so, at the moment anyway, and yet, sitting against that tree, nibbling chocolate in the darkness amid intense silence, I experienced a kaleidoscope of memories. My life had been a somewhat uneventful one up to 1938 and it was while in the service of the LNE Railway Company in a clerical capacity that a fellow clerk and myself fell to discussing what we would do when war came, as it surely would. Thinking along the lines of the unpleasant experiences of infantrymen in the First World War, we decided the Royal Air Force would be a cleaner way of life (or death), whichever way one thought, and so it was that I joined the RAF in 1940. Everyone wanted to be a pilot of course, but it was not to be, and I was accepted as a wireless operator.

Training started at Blackpool and mostly consisted of square bashing and rifle drill on the promenade or in the side streets, plus occasional morse code training periods, up to six words per minute, in the cold confines of South Shore tram sheds.

I remembered being billeted with six or seven other bods in a commandeered guest-house where we were served beans on toast for breakfast every day, for the six weeks we spent in Blackpool. We were supposed to get at least one egg per week, but were informed, in no uncertain terms by our landlady that this was a fallacy, we were not 'entitled' to anything.

The course at Blackpool was followed by more advanced training at Yatesbury, a large straggling camp on the bleak Wiltshire Downs. Life here had its ups and downs, four of us who palled up together being 'adopted' by a business couple who owned a shop in Marlborough and where we spent some pleasant weekends.

After Yatesbury came Gunnery School in Scotland, after which we were awarded our half wing as WOP/AGs and posted to Operational Training at Kinloss, and it was here that I met Hillier and Canter, eventually crewing up with them and arriving at Linton-on-Ouse.

Why those thoughts should permeate my mind in this extraordinary and still unreal situation, I have no idea. Perhaps it was the very suddenness of the change in my fortunes which triggered them off.

Anyway, with that medley of thoughts crowding my mind, I fell asleep.

CHAPTER THREE

A Lucky Contact

I awoke suddenly, not immediately aware of where I was, but feeling intensely cold. Very close to me, I could hear rustling in the undergrowth accompanied by snuffling noises and frequent grunts. I looked at my watch. It was 4.30 a.m. and still very dark. I had slept for over six hours and now felt so frozen that it was difficult to move. The rustling continued and I thought I saw a movement across the path opposite me. I put it down to an illusion or trick of my eyes after awaking suddenly. But no, there it was again, another movement and a louder grunt. Suddenly it dawned on me, they were boars, wild boars and I had been asleep among them for six hours.

Hastily and painfully, I scrambled to my feet and the movement must have disconcerted the beasts, because the rustling and grunting became louder as they made off into the darkness of the forest.

Hell, I was cold. I flapped my arms, energetically rubbed my leg muscles, tried running on the spot, and after a while felt the circulation painfully return to my limbs. It must have been the proximity of the boars that woke me up, which was probably a good thing, because I think if I had slept much longer in that temperature I might never have awakened at all. After all, it was December, and my only clothing was the woollen flying underwear, uniform shirt, white polo-neck sweater, battledress blouse and slacks, silk inner gloves, forage cap and flying boots.

I nibbled another biscuit, decided to get moving again in an attempt to get out of the forest and try to locate where I was, and set off once more along the main path through the trees. Occasionally I heard the sound of aircraft overhead, German no doubt, then I heard a dog barking, but it seemed to be a considerable distance away. After a further few minutes, I again heard the barking and thought, God, I hope they're not

44

searching the area with dogs. I heard nothing more for about half an hour, when suddenly the path emerged from the trees into open country. The dawn light was appearing in the east and through the dimness I could discern fields, hedges and walls. The path continued slightly down hill now, with nothing on either side but flat fields, and still heading in a roughly westerly direction.

I had to be doubly careful now, out in the open country, and particularly so, since the sky was getting lighter, and very soon it would be daylight. Instructions were to move by night and lie up during daylight hours, but I was only just beginning to feel warm again, so I carried on at a brisk pace but nevertheless keeping a sharp look-out. As it became steadily lighter, I was able to see that the surrounding countryside was of a gently rolling nature, a mixture of pasture and agricultural land, dotted here and there with copses and larger patches of woodland. Looking back, the woodland or forest from which I emerged, seemed to be very extensive indeed and I was more than relieved to have left it, and its somewhat disturbing occupants, behind me.

Very soon, I was approaching a T-junction with what was obviously more of a major road than the one by which I had left the forest. There was no sign of pedestrian or vehicular traffic within seeing distance, in either direction, and as I cautiously approached the junction, I was delighted to see a signpost. One arm, pointing to the right, read Rupt-devant St Mihiel, the other Rumont and Grimecourt. Thank God, I breathed, at least I'm in France. Rumont and Grimecourt meant nothing to me geographically, but St Mihiel rang a bell. Having read books on the 1914–18 war, I remembered that the town of St Mihiel was the furthest point of advance of American troops before the cease fire was declared in 1918. It was in Lorraine, the eastern province of France, which together with Alsace had previously been annexed by Germany during the Franco-Prussian war of 1870. Rupt-devant-St-Mihiel would probably be a small village below St Mihiel. I hastily got out my silk map and soon located the area where I was. Commercy to the south-east, St Mihiel roughly east by north, and Bar-le-Duc to the west, all fairly large towns and to be avoided at all costs.

I took the road towards Rumont and Grimecourt, again in a westerly direction, disobeying all the rules about avoiding main roads and travelling only by night, but keeping a sharp lookout and listening intently for any sound of engines, airborne or otherwise. Now I knew I was in France, I hoped that, should I meet or be approached by anyone, the chances were it would be a French civilian, who might be able to help. I surmised that I was hardly likely to meet a German soldier walking alone along a country road, and if there was a German column en route, I would no doubt hear or see their approach in sufficient time to conceal myself behind the hedge which bordered the road.

As I walked, I pondered on the long-term possibilities of the future. It was, at least, 200 kilometres to Paris from this part of France, then another 200 kilometres to the Channel coast, and apart from the distances involved, the journey would be thwart with difficulties in German-occupied territory. I would have to have help of some kind or another, and I reckoned this depended upon initiative on my part, aided by oodles of luck, mainly the latter. Already I was very much aware that flying boots, comfortable and warm in an aircraft, were not the ideal footware for long-distance walking, so I gradually came to the conclusion that I had to take the chance, that any French civilian whom I might approach, would prove amenable.

A further instruction, we, as aircrew, received at escape and survival lectures was, if we came upon a house, farm or village, and had decided upon trying to obtain assistance, we should watch the place from safe concealment, and for as long as possible, note anything suspicious, and generally satisfy ourselves that the place could reasonably be considered safe, mainly from the point of view of absence of German soldiery and passage of military traffic. Only then should we appeal for help, trusting that the occupants were sympathetic to our predicament. This then would be my short-term plan.

I walked for a good half hour, when I heard again the sound of an engine or engines and moved off the road into the shelter of the bordering hedgerows and bushes. The noise developed into the deep-throated roar of a motorcycle combination with two steel-helmeted soldiers aboard, the rifle of the driver slung across his back and his passenger sitting in the sidecar holding his upright in front of him. They passed with a staccato of back-firing, clouds of dirty black smoke pouring from the exhaust, and very obviously in need of a major service or overhaul. They were heading in the same direction of

Grimecourt and Rumont. I emerged from concealment and, after only a few minutes, another engine was heard heading in the same direction. This time it was a grey camouflaged open car containing two German officers. I reckoned it was time to leave this road and so as I had been instructed: take to the fields, hedges and woods. This I did, experiencing difficulty crossing ditches, forcing unpleasant hedges and getting pretty wet around the legs in the undergrowth and bracken, where overnight frost was now melting.

It was now almost broad daylight, with every indication of a bright sunny day ahead, not that that enthralled me very much. I could still see the road running parallel to my route, and traffic was getting more frequent now. Eventually I could see that, a short way ahead, the road forked, and I stopped in the shelter of a small copse watching the traffic flow. Without exception, all the vehicles carried straight on, nothing at all turned on to the minor road to the left. I set off again, veering away from the main road and headed in the direction of the minor road, still keeping to the fields. Eventually the ground began to fall away towards a small river, which I later found to be named the Aire. The only means of crossing seemed to be by a stone bridge just short of the small hamlet of Grimecourt. I crossed, without event, and again took to the fields, hedges and ditches. By now, I must have looked as though I had been pulled through more than one hedge backwards; my uniform trousers were ripped in places, and wet, and my hands covered in scratches and cuts from the various thorns and brambles encountered in ditches and undergrowth. Furthermore, I was thirsty and not a little despondent. Seeing across the fields to my right another, larger, village, I carefully made my way towards it, and considered it for an hour or more. It seemed to be very quiet with only an odd person appearing now and again into and out of the houses and gardens bordering the only part of a village street I could see.

This is it, I thought, nothing ventured, nothing gained. Leaving my hiding place I walked across the fields to the village. The nearest house was somewhat isolated from the larger group of dwellings forming the village street, and my direction from the fields led me to the rear of the house, where a lady was just about to enter the door from the back garden.

I called, 'Madame.'

She turned and looked at me, a look of apprehension appeared in her eyes and she hastily entered the house, firmly shutting the door behind her. I pressed on and knocked on the door.

'*Madame,*' I called, '*J'ai soif. Puis-je avoir de l'eau?*'

The accent, of course, was attrocious, my French being only what I learned at school ten years previously.

From behind the closed door she shouted:

'*Non, non, monsieur! Allez, allez.*'

She seemed almost hysterical, but I persisted and in the best French I could muster, explained that I had been out all night in the forest and walked all morning, was very thirsty and all I needed was one drink and I should be on my way. But it was no use.

'Go away, please go away,' she shouted.

I gave up, and moved away round to the front of the house and the village street. Looking back I saw her face at the front window peeping through the curtains, willing me away. She was quite an old lady, with grey wispy hair straggling her forehead, and obviously scared out of her wits, perhaps at my scarecrow appearance, or because she realised what I was. Later, I found out that she was somewhat retarded mentally, had little or nothing to do with her neighbours, and was virtually a recluse.

I walked the short length of the village street and came upon a metal water trough with a pump operated by the old-fashioned pump handle. I stopped, operated the handle, drank some water, using my hands as a cup, then leaned over the trough and commenced splashing water onto my face and hair.

As I performed these rough ablutions, I suddenly had a feeling that I was not alone, and being watched. I half turned, not raising my head and saw two pairs of legs, immediately behind me, and one pair was encased in leggings and dark olive green uniform breeches. A uniform was the last thing in the world I wanted to see.

Hell, I thought, now what? My gaze travelled upwards taking in a uniform tunic with belt and a green beret surmounting a fresh-coloured young face. German soldiery didn't wear dark green uniform, neither did they wear berets, so what was he? His companion, a much older man, puffing at a pipe, was nondescriptly dressed, more like a farmer type. The younger person spoke, looking hard at my inside-out tattered blouse:

'*Où allez vous?*'

I didn't answer, and turned back to the water trough.

'*Vous êtes un soldat,*' he continued, more of a statement of fact than a question, and in a very quiet reassuring voice. This is the opportunity, I inwardly thought, and turning towards the couple:

'*Non. Je suis –*' I began.

'*Vous êtes RAF,*' interrupted the younger person. '*Vous êtes anglais.*' Again, not a question, but a definite statement of fact, as he scrutinised my clothing.

'*Oui,*' I replied. '*Je suis un aviateur anglais.*'

This was the moment, no hesitation now. Whatever was to come must be faced. There was no turning back.

The young man spoke again in a more urgent tone, and *in English*:

'Come quickly,' pointing across the road. Then his hand was on my arm in a fast grip above the elbow, and in a moment I was propelled across the street into a house opposite the trough. The older man glanced up and down the road and quickly followed, bolting the door behind him.

I was in a large stone flagged kitchen-cum-living room with a table in the centre, around which were a few wooden chairs. Beyond this, stairs led upward, and to the left was a door. There was a movement overhead, as if in the room above, and then the creaking of the stairs.

'*Qui est là?*'

I turned and faced the stairs, seeing a little elderly lady with bright eyes and a kindly smile come towards me. She reached up, grasped my shoulders with both hands, and kissed me on both cheeks, and then held me at arm's length.

'*Vous parlez français?*'

'*Non,*' I replied, '*seulement un petit peu.*'

'*N'importe,*' she said, '*Fernand parle anglais très bien.*'

She had seen me, from an upstairs window, arrive at the trough, watched all my antics, had at once realised what I was, and sent the two Frenchmen out to speak to me.

There now appeared from the door on the left of the room two more French women, one about the same age as the younger of the two men, and the other a year or two older. A few rapid words of French were exchanged, which apparently explained to them the situation, and I was subjected to wide-eyed stares of curiosity.

I was made to sit down at the simple wooden table, where suddenly long sticks of dark brown French bread appeared, together with cheese and bottles of red wine. The atmosphere was celebratory and party-like. I was certainly among friends. I was informed that the name of the village was Levoncourt in the department of the Meuse. The older man, whose house this was, was called Robert Verdun and his wife Jeanne. The younger of the other two French women was Georgette their daughter and fiancée of Fernand Cherrier, the young man, who was employed in the Department de l'Eau et Forêts, something like our present Forestry Commission. This explained the uniform which had previously worried me somewhat.

I tucked into the bread and cheese, with gusto, whilst my glass was continually being topped up with red wine. The conversation was much too rapid for me to follow in detail, but it was obvious they were discussing me, and it was necessary for me to hide pro-tem. I, in turn, explained to Fernand, in a mixture of French and English, what had happened since the previous evening, the forest, the boars, the German transport I had seen, and the episode with the old lady in the house further back in the village. The forest where I had landed was evidently called the Forêt de Koers and the resident population of boars were quite harmless in fact. The German transport would be passing from Verdun or St Mihiel to Bar-le-Duc and St Dizier where there was a German night fighter base. The fighter who shot us down came from the base. Fernand also explained that the villagers had heard the gunfire of the previous evening and seen the flames from the doomed aircraft, as it gradually lost height going north, but were unable to see the parachutes descending, due to the darkness. Already Fernand had made it his business to find out where the aircraft had finally crashed; in a wood near Pierrefitte-sur-Aire, about 15 kms north of Levoncourt, and the pilot and rear gunner had been killed. Hillier, I found out later was badly burned around the lower half of the body, and how he had failed to get out, I shall never know. Smithy, the rear gunner, had attempted to bale out of the turret, in the orthodox way, but his canopy and shroud

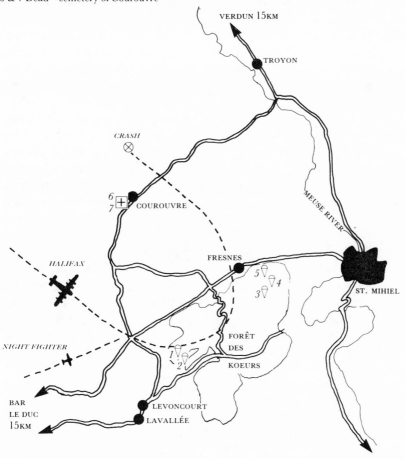

December 6th-7th 1942

Scale: 1cm=2km

1 & 2 Escaped via Levoncourt & Lavallée
3, 4 & 5 Prisoners – taken at Fresnes
6 & 7 Dead – cemetery of Courouvre

VERDUN 15KM

TROYON

CRASH

6
7 COUROUVRE

MEUSE RIVER

HALIFAX

FRESNES

5
3 4

ST. MIHIEL

FORÊT
DES
KOEURS

NIGHT FIGHTER

1
2

BAR
LE DUC
15KM

LEVONCOURT
LAVALLÉE

Map based on that drawn by M. Fernand Cherrier at Levoncourt after the war: his interpretation of the action on the night of 6 December 1942.

lines became entangled with the turret or tail assembly, and he was hanging helplessly from the aircraft until it crashed. Of the remainder of the crew there was, as yet, no trace, except for myself.

I continued to tuck into the bread and cheese with relish. This was my first taste of the so-called wartime black bread, and actually it was delicious, freshly baked too. Very soon, frequent knocks sounded on the front door; people were carefully being admitted and soon the kitchen was full of villagers. People other than Madame Verdun had observed events at the water trough and natural village curiosity prevailed, to see who the stranger was. When they were enlightened of the fact that I was an '*aviateur anglais*' they brimmed over with pleasure, all wanting to exchange the usual French greetings of kisses on both cheeks and handshakes. Some even returned to their homes and came back with more wine and cheese, which they pressed upon me, chattering all the time in rapid French, among themselves and to me, it never occurring to them that I could only understand a word or two here and there. The excitement was terrific, and temporarily I forgot my troubles, and thought, at this rate, and with all this friendliness, I'll be on my way home in no time at all. On this score, I was sadly mistaken, of course, but nevertheless the occasion was to be the beginning of my eventual salvation.

It soon became apparent that my appearance in the village was momentous, and an event to be celebrated fully. All my previous doubts about the immediate future were dispelled by the boisterous enthusiasm now surrounding me. The precariousness of the situation, was either not realised by the family, or was being purposely ignored, and temporarily, I also forgot about the serious consequences which could result from the proceedings, should the Germans get to know about it.

Fernand was so optimistic about the fate of the rest of the crew, that he had me convinced that they would eventually turn up. He plied me with questions about bombing operations over Germany, said how they listened every night to hear the bombers passing overhead towards Germany 'in order to do their good workings', as he put it. They had a radio in the village, he said, and they listened to the BBC as much as they could, but batteries were difficult to obtain. There were many Germans in St Mihiel, Bar-le-Duc and Commercy, but the surrounding villages were rarely bothered by them. He and the family were undoubtedly excited and pleased to receive me. No RAF aircraft had been brought down so close to this village. The only other aircraft to be brought down had been near Laneuville/Meuse, in April 1940, and two crew had been killed. This village was north of Verdun, and quite some distance from Levoncourt. He didn't know the type of aircraft either, or whether there had been any survivors.

Everyone wanted to know where I lived in England and what kind of countryside it was. Was I married, were my parents alive? What kind of work did I do? How were we standing up to German air raids and was there much damage? All the conversation was carried on in a mixture of French and English and I reckon I learned to speak and understand more French in half an hour than I ever learned at school in a month.

In due course, Fernand, who obviously was held in esteem and possessed some authority in the community in spite of his youth, (he was only nineteen) managed to persuade everyone to leave and suggested that I should get some rest whilst he went to try and find my parachute in the forest. Above the bedrooms on the first floor, was a loft reached by a ladder into which he shepherded me, and where I could bed down in the straw and get some undisturbed sleep. With an encouraging grin he left me and I heard him descend the ladder.

I didn't sleep immediately, but lay listening to the low murmur of conversation coming from downstairs, and marvelling at this unexpected stroke of luck which had befallen me so soon, but saddened about Bill Hillier and Smithy. I couldn't convince myself that they were dead. Perhaps the information was incorrect and the aircraft containing the two bodies wasn't ours, but some other Halifax shot down that evening. After all Bill was OK when I jumped and in perfect control of the Halifax. Smithy, I hadn't heard from on the intercom, but there was no reason to believe he hadn't successfully got out of the turret, and where were the other four? With these thoughts in my mind and influenced no doubt by the fair quantity of wine which I had consumed, I nodded off.

I came to with a start, awakened by the sound of the door latch of the loft being raised. The door opened and framed in the opening was Fernand, beaming all over his face, and another figure half hidden behind him. Fernand moved into the loft and stood aside allowing his companion to enter.

It was Eddy! Eddie Canter, navigator of 'P' Popsie, looking like me, somewhat worse for wear but still in one piece.

'Hello, Robbie,' he said. 'Good to see you! You OK?' He stepped forward and shook my hand and grinned somewhat morosely. Emotion was not one of Eddy's strong points, and even on this occasion there was no trace of it. For my part, I could hardly contain myself or believe this second lucky break, and literally grabbed him round the shoulders and hugged him towards me.

'God, I'm glad to see you,' I cried. 'Where are the rest of them?'

Before he could answer, Fernand intervened and suggested we go downstairs. In the living room we sat round the table again, and this time a bottle of Cognac appeared. ' *Vive la RAF,*' said Fernand.

'*Vive la France,*' we replied.

Fernand then related to us that about half an hour after I had been seen at the trough, hustled into the house and bedded down in the loft, a German motorcycle patrol had descended upon the village demanding to know whether any English aviators had been seen in the village or surrounding countryside.

No one of course knew anything of any airmen, or even that a plane had been shot down and the Germans pointed out in no uncertain terms, the penalties for assisting enemy aircrews or withholding information which would lead to their capture. They then pushed off in the direction of Grimecourt. Evidently the hunt was on!

Fernand was not in the least perturbed, but admitted we had had a lucky escape, the patrol arriving during the period between the time of my arrival and Eddy subsequently entering the village sometime later. Briefly, I repeated my story for Eddy's benefit, after which he related his experience. He had landed in the same forest, but high up in a tree and found himself suspended by his canopy cords from a tree branch at an unknown height from the ground. In an effort to estimate the drop he let fall his plastic escape pack and listened for it to hit the ground. He judged the height to be reasonable, pressed the quick release button of his harness and fell free. Unfortunately the escape pack had struck a tree branch before falling into the undergrowth, giving a false impression of his height, and he actually fell nearly twenty feet and landed pretty heavily, but fortunately without serious injury. He retrieved his escape pack without trouble but could do nothing about the parachute canopy and harness which were still hanging from the tree branches, well out of his reach. Fernand found the parachute the following evening, but was unable to locate mine, which of course I had hidden in the undergrowth.

Canter spent more time than I had done in the forest, trying to locate the rest of the crew and like me frequently had to avoid unknown pedestrians and cyclists and had also heard the sound of transport but had never actually seen any vehicles. He had moved through the forest in more or less the same direction as myself, probably on a parallel course, discovered eventually that he was on French soil rather than German and finally by pure coincidence arrived on the outskirts of Levoncourt and met Fernand, at the moment setting off to try to find my parachute. Fernand recognised immediately that this was obviously another crew member and hurried him back to the house explaining to him that I was already there, safe and unhurt.

The conversation, in a mixture of French and English continued round the table in the kitchen and Fernand told us that he was a junior member of the Department de l'Eau et Forêts and was learning the job. We gathered that he was a sort of apprentice. After the war he rose to the rank of Chief Inspector in the Department of the Meuse and retired as such in 1983. He is now Mayor of Troyon; a village between Bar-le-Duc and Verdun.

He repeated, that up to now, they had not been bothered much at Levoncourt by the Germans although in the towns of Bar-le-Duc, Commercy and St Mihiel, troops were very much in evidence, but were acting decorously towards the residents. We would therefore be quite safe for a short while until 'arrangements' could be made to get us back to England. The way he spoke certainly allayed our fears and gave us valuable comfort and confidence. He was sure that it would be the simplest thing in the world to get us back to our squadron, but he was subsequently to learn that it was not so easy. After all, we were the first RAF personnel he had encountered, and the

Resistance and escape procedures were in their infancy at this time in this area. There were to be another 27 RAF aircraft shot down in this small department of the Meuse before the end of the war, by which time, a lot had been learned about the successful evacuation of surviving crew members.

Later that evening after a wash and clean up we left the house together with Fernand and the other members of the family and were taken to Fernand's home, only a short distance away, in the same village and introduced to his parents. It was here that we had our first sit-down meal in France. As in England, food was rationed, but you wouldn't have thought so judging by the fare we consumed that evening. How they managed it we never found out; and the meal lasted, like most French meals, well into the late evening and terminated with real coffee and homemade liqueurs.

It had been arranged that we would sleep that night at Fernand's home, where there was a spare room and eventually we were able to take advantage of the large double bed already made up for us, where almost convinced by the events of the day that we would be home within a day or two, we slept soundly.

CHAPTER FOUR

The Cherrier Family

It was late morning when we awoke, and for quite a while I lay uncertain as to where I was in this strange unfamiliar room in a strange house and in a foreign country, an enemy-occupied foreign country, at that. Then with a glow of gratitude I remembered, as Madame Cherrier, Fernand's mother, came in with a jug of coffee and cups. While we were drinking, Fernand came up and sat on the edge of the bed. It would not be advisable, he explained, for us to venture outside at the moment in case more German patrols were active, looking for any survivors and we should remain in the bedroom till further notice. He left one or two books and magazines and a game of draughts and told us he intended continuing his interrupted journey into the forest to find the parachutes, and possibly to learn something about the crash and maybe the whereabouts of our comrades. As it was, the village was not troubled again that day by German search patrols and eventually Fernand returned having found Eddy's parachute hanging in the trees, fortunately before the Germans found it. He had no news of other survivors but had learned that Hillier and Smith were to be buried that afternoon in the little village cemetery of Courouvre, a short distance away from where the bomber had crashed.

After the war when I visited Fernand, we went to the little cemetery to see the graves which were and still are well looked after by the villagers. We learned from one Frenchman and his wife, M. and Mme Perignon, who remembered the occasion very well, that on the afternoon of the internment, a small detachment of German soldiers arrived and performed the honours of a military funeral over the graves. The Luftwaffe pilot of the fighter who shot us down was also present and expressed his regrets remarking to M. Perignon in good French:

'*Aujourd-hui les deux, peut-etre demain, moi!*' translated to mean, today it is those two perhaps tomorrow me!

Needless to say, the village later received a less pleasant visit from civilian-clothed SS personnel demanding information regarding two other members of the crew of the bomber, still unaccounted for. Apparently the other three chaps had turned up in the village of Fresnes-au-Mont, Johnny Parkin with a broken ankle, and promptly turned over to the Germans by the Mayor of that village to become prisoners of war.

But, back to Levoncourt. Fernand then informed us that he and his family were taking us back to his fiancée's home where we would have '*déjeuner*' (lunch). As we walked back to the little house opposite the trough, the curious eyes of many villagers followed us. One or two, bolder perhaps than the others, insisted on coming across from their homes to shake hands and kiss us once again. I doubt very much whether there had ever been before such excitement in this little village. I wondered whether they actually realised how potentially dangerous the occasion was, and the harsh treatment that would be meted out if ever the German authorities discovered what had taken place. Brave or ignorant? The former I prefer to believe.

We reached the home of the Verduns, and were straight away welcomed effusively and sat down to apéritifs. During apéritifs we were joined by Georgette's brother and his wife, who also lived in the village, thus making up a party of ten of us for lunch. Once more we ate well enjoying the company and conversation which centred mostly on exchanges of our family life at home in England and our friends' family lives in France. They were most interested to learn of life on a bomber station in England, and to see at first hand our uniforms, flying kit, various escape aids, badges and buttons etc. For the duration of the meal, even for the duration of that day it was difficult to believe that this was wartime France, it seemed more like a normal luncheon party with well known close friends.

During the afternoon Fernand reckoned it safe to pay one or two visits to close friends of the family living in the village, and they were all highly delighted and excited to take part in what they considered to be a 'momentous' occasion.

We partook of the evening meal, once again at the home of Fernand's parents. Here we were given civilian type smocks and berets which we exchanged for our battle dress blouses and caps; trousers couldn't be found but two pairs of boots were obtained, which were a reasonable fit and we parted with our flying boots. I also left with Fernand my escape pack, one or two English coins and photographs – all of these he kept throughout the remainder of the war and he produced them, when I made my first visit to France in 1948.

He was so proud of the flying boots, that he wore them one day in the town of Bar-le-Duc. While looking in a shop window, he saw in the glass the reflection of two German officers on the opposite side of the street, one of whom seemed to be observing his footwear suspiciously and pointing them out to his companion. Fernand, realising his silly venture, beat a hasty retreat into and through the side streets of the town and fortunately got away with it.

We would sleep the night at Fernand's and on the morrow would be taken to another village close by, where Fernand said he had good friends with whom we would stay for the day and night, before we were set on our way – to England? It was as though an aircraft was expected to land, which we would board and fly back to our squadron without further ado. Such was the impression given us by our courageous French helpers.

We said our goodnights to the family and attempted in some very inadequate words to express our appreciation for their kindness and all they were doing in spite of the risk involved.

'*Bonsoir, mes amis. Dormez bien.*'

'*Bonsoir et vous aussi,*' we replied and climbed the stairs and got into bed.

Warm, fed and feeling reasonably secure we should have dropped off immediately but this was not the case. Both of us lay awake thinking and talking of the risks to which these brave people were subjecting themselves on our behalf, and fell to debating what our reaction would be, if by some misfortune we were captured, wearing part civilian clothing and interrogated regarding how we had procured the clothing and who had helped us. We still carried our service identity tags and technically, if we were captured, should be treated as prisoners of war, divulging only name, rank and number. However this depended much upon by whom we were captured, the military authorities or the hated Gestapo. The latter were infamous for using more persuasive measures to extract information and neither of us could visualise how we would react should the worst happen. They were disturbing thoughts and it was quite a while before we eventually slept. During the whole of my sojourn in France this was my only fear, and the problem was always uppermost in my mind.

The following morning we came down to breakfast of coffee and bread rolls, and wearing the articles of civilian clothing which had been provided. Both Fernand and his parents remarked on how authentic I looked in my black smock and beret, my dark hair and moustache being typically French. They were not so sure about Canter, who was naturally of a fair complexion and rather Anglo-Saxon in appearance. One asset we both had, however basic it was: we could both speak and understand French reasonably well, probably as good as or maybe better than many Germans. The main danger was lack of identity cards and papers.

The village to which we were to go that day, was only one and a half kilometres distant, and was called Lavallée and we said a further goodbye to our friends, before setting off with Fernand walking to Lavallée. Reaching the village we passed over a little arched bridge and on the far side sitting on a stone parapet, was a dark clad figure whom Fernand immediately hailed and exchanged the usual greetings. This gentleman dressed in the long black-skirted habit of a priest was M. Jean Ançelot, curé of St Julien, near Commercy, who lived in a large detached house on the edge of the village, which served as what we call in England a manse or vicarage. M. Ançelot was a thin man of medium height with dark complexion, close-cropped black hair, very penetrating eyes and wore rimless spectacles. He was hatless and over his close-fitting black habit hung a rosary.

Fernand introduced us and since the priest expressed no surprise I'm sure he was expecting us to arrive at that time, Fernand having probably put him in the picture beforehand. The greeting was warm and friendly, and I was particularly surprised at the strength of this man's grip when we shook hands. For a man of his stature and build, his grip was very firm. He gestured to his house a few yards beyond the little bridge, and we followed Fernand and the priest up three steps leading to the large front entrance and into a spacious hall, very sparsely furnished. From here we passed into a large, high-ceilinged dining room, containing a heavy refectory table around which were similarly heavy, high-backed dining chairs. On one wall was a large bookcase, against the other stood a massive carved sideboard reaching nearly to the ceiling and the room was pleasantly warmed by a solid fuel stove. A window looked out upon a tree enclosed garden, to the rear of the house.

We all sat down at the long table and through a door which evidently led into the kitchen came a small lady, bearing the inevitable bottle of wine, glasses and a plate of plain biscuits. This was the curé's housekeeper, and we were introduced to her, no effort being made to conceal the fact that we were British flyers. She was invited to sit down and join us. The drinks were poured, the usual toasts proposed with a clinking of glasses, after which the curé looked quizzically at both of us, enquiring whether we had thought of any future contingency plans. Eddy replied that we hadn't and that our instructions were, if we found ourselves in friendly hands to leave all arrangements to the persons concerned and follow any advice given, without question, however doubtful it may appear at the time.

M. Ancelot then proceeded to explain that, as well as being the spiritual leader of the large community living in the various villages surrounding the town of Commercy, he was also *Chef de Résistance* of a small group of Frenchmen in the area who were eagerly taking every opportunity to embarrass the local occupying forces in anyway they could, and this would naturally include assisting and finding shot down airmen. We were the first two airmen to have arrived in this particular area so he now enthusiastically welcomed the opportunity to put this into practice. Fernand, his family and his fiancée's family were naturally all ardent supporters, and only too happy to lend their help to the group. Later in the war the group became very active indeed, as the bomber offensive was increased and more and more aircrews needed assistance to evade successfully in this area of France, and more than a few, courageous Frenchmen paid the penalty for such activities during the ensuing years.

The curé continued to explain that in his opinion the best way out of France was via Spain, a long, long journey he agreed, but much more feasible than to attempt a return via the coast and English Channel, where security and defences would be formidable. So the first part of our journey would be to reach Paris, where resistance and underground operations were now becoming effective. Various types and sizes of maps were produced and pored over by the four of us, and we were advised of a route to take to reach a village where the curé knew there was a 'safe house' and where further help would be available. We would remain there, in this house, with the curé and his housekeeper, sleep here that night, and make our departure the following morning.

Once again we dined well, this time all credit for a satisfying meal being due to M. Ančelot's housekeeper who served us soup, followed by luscious boiled ham with varied choice of vegetables which were served from hot pots on the kitchen stove. Salad, followed by a delicious trifle and fresh fruit, ended what could only be called a mini banquet. In due course coffee and cognac appeared, prolonging the session until nearly 10.30 pm. M. Ançelot took us up to a bedroom containing a large double bed, on which was the most enormous brilliant red duvet, I had ever seen. It was like a large balloon but extremely light in weight and we found that it kept the bed cosily warm despite the room temperature, which was pretty low, since there was no heating upstairs.

We were awakened before daybreak, the following morning by Madame, the housekeeper entering the room with two steaming hot bowls of coffee, and telling us that the curé and Fernand, who had arrived early from Levoncourt, would await while we drank and dressed. Quickly we did as requested, came down to the dining room where we partook of bread rolls and further coffee. A 1/100,000 map had been left out on the table, covering the route from Lavallée to a village called Brabant-le-Roi wherein was the safe house referred to by the curé the previous evening. We were briefed on this map, and advised the route to take avoiding the major town of Bar-le-Duc and the larger villages near or on the line of our route, and given directions to enable us to find the 'safe house'.

No mention was made of the names of the people who were to help us since there existed many collaborators who were quite willing to inform to the Germans, even to the extent of betraying their friends and neighbours either for financial reward or preferential treatment. People were therefore hesitant to exchange names until they were very, very, certain

Levoncourt, par Villotte s/Aire
Meuse, France

February 4th. 1912

Mr. & Mrs. H.O. Robertson,

There are now, more than two years ago, exactly on December 7th 1942, that a "Hallifax" machine was shot down by a German night-fighter, a few miles farther than our village. A day later, we had the visit of your husband, Harry and another member of the bomber.

Two days after, after changing clothes, they left our village and took the direction of their home.

We received a letter from Paris a week later telling us they were in good health and ready to fly again to England.

Since, we heard nothing about our friends. I hoped a message through B.B.C. But nothing.

Now, that our country has been liberated by the glorious Allied troops, I am glad to write to you, in order to receive some news about Harry.

Is he always in the R.A.F.?

We hear, but every night, the terrific noise of thousand and thousand "Hallifax" and "Lancaster" bombers, passing over our heads, and flying to Germany in order to do their good working, and we think that Harry can be in one of those squadrons.

The first page of Fernand Cherrier's letter to me after the liberation. (He has dated it wrongly).

of one another. Even then, it was considered better to be anonymous, since if a name was not known, then it couldn't be given away under duress, should a person be arrested and interrogated.

Also on the table was a small knapsack containing bread, cheese and fruit, and a box of matches. We were offered a small amount of money also, but this we politely refused since our escape packs contained a sum of Belgian and French francs, for just such an occasion. I had kept the money when I left my pack with Fernand the previous day. We were also supplied with forged work permits and ration permits also forged.

On a final note, Fernand asked if when we got back home, we would send a message through the BBC, saying 'The swallows have returned', which would indicate our safe arrival. We promised, and did request this, at our debriefing but nothing ever came of it, I am sorry to say. After brief farewells, handshakes and bidding us *bon chance*, we left our friends and we were on our way:

It was Thursday, 10th December, five days after having been shot down.

At Blackpool whilst on preliminary training in 1941. I am front right.

Fernand Cherrier with members of his family just after the war, outside the house where they sheltered me. They were all involved in our evasion at Levoncourt.

Monsieur and Madame Cherrier when they stayed with my wife and myself in England in 1960.

Left Monsieur Jean Ançelot, curé of St Julien. He and his housekeeper hid us in Lavallee for one night prior to our departure for Brabant.

Below The house of Monsieur Jean Ançelot, curé of St Julien. It was from this doorway that we left in early morning darkness for Brabant-le-Roe, and the supposed 'safe house'.

Right Odette Mailland, who assisted us at Rancourt-sur-Ornain.

Below The café in rue St Claude, Paris, where we first made contact with Monsieur Roussel and the Resistance cell.

Below right Monsieur Roussel, Odette's uncle, who together with Yves Chardac and others hid us in various parts of Paris before taking us south to Ruffec and Madame Denivelle. He is outside 15 rue St Claude.

With Yves Chardac in Paris in 1949.

Gaston Denivelle of Ruffec in the courtyard at the rear of the house where we were hidden. The hanging baskets in the background are the helmets of German soldiers he killed in a desperate gun-battle in this yard in 1944.

Gaston Denivelle.

Madame Renée Denivelle.

CHAPTER FIVE

A Not So 'Safe House'

It was hardly daylight when we started and the village of Brabant was approximately thirty kilometres distant. Even allowing for possible diversions, we had ample time to reach it before darkness returned that evening. The first three to four miles were covered in about an hour and we reached the first village of Erize-St Dizier by which time it was daylight, with the promise of good weather. It was very cold and frost covered the hedges and fields, but the sun was shining in a cloudless sky and, as yet, we had seen no signs of life. The road from here turned right, signposted to Rumont and I remembered when I had come out of the Forêt de Koers, seen my first signpost, checked out my map, I noticed that most traffic of a military nature headed for Rumont, then probably Bar-le-Duc. I mentioned this to Eddy, and after about one kilometre, we veered left off the road into fields and distant woodland, in the direction of Vavincourt and avoided Rumont.

Here we were in pretty open country and soon perceived we were approaching a main road, the main road leading from Rumont, which we had previously by-passed, to Bar-le-Duc, further to the south. There was a fair amount of traffic passing along this main road but once across it, there were the beginnings of a large wood within a few yards. We chose a point where a good view was obtainable in either direction, and when the opportunity arose, made a quick dash across and gained the cover of the wood. We moved through the wood, parallel to the minor road which skirted it, and led in the direction of Vavincourt and emerged once more into open country.

Walking along a hedge, Eddy leading, we came to a gate which gave us the direction we wanted, and hesitated when we saw some movement ahead of us. We quickly reversed, re-climbed the gate and started down the other side of the hedge, first walking then running whilst a raucous shout echoed across the field. We stopped about half a kilometre further on and listened intently, but there was no sign of pursuit. We discussed the situation and decided there and then that we were becoming too complacent, and that the business we were in allowed for no relaxation from watching for the unexpected change in events which were liable to occur.

Half an hour later we were approaching Vavincourt and decided it would be discreet to by-pass the place. It was just as well we did, because we learned later that there was an anti-aircraft unit stationed there. Leaving Vavincourt, still in open country, we were soon in the cover of a much larger forest through which ran a railway line. We crossed without any trouble and soon came to the further edge of the forest. Here we ran unexpectedly into a throng of youths dressed in grey, possibly men from a German Forestry Camp. Busy felling trees and piling wood, they appeared to take no notice as we passed them. A sudden shout from one of the men in charge tended to make us want to turn round, which might have invited suspicion. We survived the temptation, and taking care not to increase our step, vaguely waved our arms in a half-hearted gesture, and pressed on through the trees. There was no second shout or any indication of anyone following us and rounding a turn in the path we breathed easier again and soon found ourselves on a small road running along the north edge of the forest into a village called Chardogne, according to our map.

Passing through without incident, at a road junction, we noted the right hand led to Laimont and Brabant-le-Roi, the left indicated Bar-le-Duc, and it was obviously a principal route. There was little cover on either side of the road for the first two kilometres, but, fortunately, only one vehicle passed us on this stretch, which we managed to avoid by hiding behind a convenient hedge. We could see ahead, another extensive wood on the right. Into this we marched and decided to investigate the contents of the knapsack since we were both decidedly peckish. We had covered approximately fifteen kilometres according to our map, about halfway to Brabant. We ate sparingly, not knowing when or how we would obtain further supplies, and I risked smoking one of my three cigarettes. There was evidence of forestry work being undertaken, but we didn't run into anyone and broke out of the wood just beyond Laimont, rejoining the road again, which at this point, had more in the way of potential concealment on the right.

It was now late afternoon, the sun was quickly sinking behind us and it would be dark by the time we reached Brabant-le-Roi. A further six kilometres brought us to the outskirts, and we crossed a bridge, the road bearing left into the village street, where we had been told the first house on the right, with a small stream running through the back garden, was our target. We waited by the bridge, taking stock of the house and its surroundings and, deciding everything seemed normal, moved towards the front of the house and Eddy knocked on the door. After a few seconds the door was opened by a woman slight in stature and with a dark complexion. As soon as she saw us a look of apprehension appeared on her face and her eyes darted to each of us in turn.

'*Oui?*' she said, in a low voice, the intonation implying a question.

'*Madame –*' began Eddy, and in the best French he could muster explained that we had been advised to come to this house, where help would be given us. She stepped back a little, and I thought that she was going to shut the door on us, but she turned her head and called,

'*Maurice!*'

A tall man came up behind her to whom she spoke in rapid French and he, in turn, surveyed us quizzically before ushering us into the house. The door opened immediately into a kitchen, where, around a heavy wooded table, were seated four other men, engaged in deep conversation. At our entry, four heads turned, and four pairs of eyes surveyed us with gazes which belied friendliness, and decidedly harboured profound suspicion. The tall man gestured us to sit down on two chairs near a large cooking range and spoke a few words to the men around the table, presumably explaining briefly the purpose and reason for our visit. There was a brief exchange of conversation between the five men, interposed with frequent glances in our direction, leaving us in no doubt, that we were the subject of the discussion. The tall man suddenly turned to us:

'Where have you come from?' he demanded. I looked questioningly at Eddy and, after a slight pause, he nodded.

'Levoncourt,' I said. 'We were shot down not far from the village.'

'Who sent you here, to this village, to this house?' Again I looked at Eddy, but got no response.

'We both arrived in Levoncourt the morning after being shot down,' I said. 'We begged a drink from an old lady living there. I don't know her name. Then we moved on into a village called Lavallée.' I didn't want to mention Fernand or his family.

'*Oui, oui*,' said the tall Frenchman, 'but who told you to come here?'

'A priest,' said Eddy.

'A priest, in Lavallée?' queried the tall man.

'Yes.'

He turned again to his companions. '*C'était le curé de St Julien. C'est bien!*' The four men looked at us with renewed interest, one of them said:

'*Vous êtes anglais, tous les deux?*'

'*Oui.*'

'*Où sont les autres?*' continued the man.

We told him that, so far as we knew, two had been killed and we didn't know anything about the other three. The atmosphere became much more relaxed and we showed our identity tags and the forged work permits and ration tickets, given us by the curé. We learned that this was the meeting place of a small group engaged in various underground activities against the Germans and the curé of St Julien was very well known by the group.

The meeting over, a simple cold meal was served and we sat at the table with the five men and the woman after which our immediate future began to be debated.

Suddenly, the sound of a car engine interrupted the proceedings, and one of the group moved towards the window which looked out from the front of the house.

'*Mon Dieu!*' he exclaimed, '*Les Allemands!*'

Chairs went over backwards as everyone was suddenly on their feet. The tall man gestured towards us. 'The back door, quickly, *allez allez!*' and as he spoke pulled, what looked like an Army Service revolver from under his jacket.

We dived across the kitchen, through the back door and into the garden, hearing as we did so, a loud banging from the front door, accompanied by raucous shouting and a scream from someone, probably the woman. Then came the sounds of shots and breaking glass as we reached a fence at the bottom of the garden, over which we scrambled. A hasty glance back to the house revealed two figures emerging from the door, backwards, firing as they came. As we continued our run, the sounds of a miniature gun battle continued from the house and back garden, gradually becoming fainter as we put more distance between us and the village.

Shortly we stopped, gasping and panting, and listened for sounds of pursuit. There were none. There was only silence, uncanny after the noise of firing. We had no idea in which direction we had been running, only aware that after the obstacle of the back garden fence, we had run down a narrow road, through a farm yard, disturbing some poultry as we galloped past, scrambled through numerous hedges and were now in an open field, or so it seemed, with no cover whatsoever.

We were virtually back to square one. The one and only contact which might have proved helpful was no longer a practical proposition. We were on our own again! What had gone wrong we wondered?

It would seem that the Germans had somehow discovered the existence of the group and their meeting place. It was an unfortunate coincidence that they had chosen to raid the place the very evening that we had arrived. They couldn't have known we were in the house. We never found out, nor did we ever find out what the result of the raid was and whether any of the Frenchmen or the woman escaped, were killed or arrested. Once again, it certainly served as a violent reminder that the business we were in was a precarious one, and those French people who were willing to help us, were in an infinitely more dangerous situation, if discovered. Nevertheless, at least we could thank providence that our luck had held insofar as we were free and not being pursued.

We reckoned that we must be within two or three kilometres of Brabant-le-Roi, judging by the distance we thought we had run, but had no idea of the direction we had taken. Eddy suggested that the premier necessity was to find somewhere to lie up and get some shut-eye, an idea which I heartily endorsed. We had walked all day, become embroiled in a miniature gun battle and run over a mile through rough country, in the dark. We needed rest.

We set off walking on a compass direction west and after negotiating a number of hedges and ditches, followed a cart track which eventually led us to a farm. There was no sign of movement, it was very quiet and no light was visible at any of

the windows of the long, low farmhouse which we could just see
in the gloom. A dog barked once, not loudly, then it whimpered.
We froze, listening for activity, but all remained quiet. A few
outbuildings were located to the right of the house, and behind
them loomed a larger building which we took to be a barn. On
investigation, this proved to be correct, and on trying the small
door, inset into the larger barn door, found it unlocked and
entered. It was even darker in the barn than outside and we
tripped and stumbled over various obstacles until our eyes
became accustomed to the darkness, and found a ladder which
led up to a hayloft through an open trap-door. Sinking
gratefully down onto the hay, we burrowed in as best we could,
in an effort to keep warm, and, in spite of the recent excitement
and escape, thoughts about the fate of the French folk at
Brabant and our own trepidations regarding the future, we fell
immediately into a deep sleep.

A hefty dig in the ribs jerked me suddenly awake, followed
by an urgent whisper, breathed by Eddy.

'Quiet, Robbie, we've got company!'

Pushing the hay aside, I sat up and listened intently. First I
heard the sound of a motor engine idling, then the sound of
voices, loud guttural voices, immediately recognisable as
German. Climbing out of the hay, I moved to the side of the
barn where the loft roof sloped almost to meet the floor and
with the aid of a Scout sheath knife which I had always worn on
my belt, managed to ease a couple of tiles free, sufficiently to
gaze out on to the farm buildings. There was a large
open-topped military lorry in the gateway, out of which were
climbing German soldiers.

There were ten of them, I counted them as they dropped out
of the lorry, plus the driver.

'It's the Boche, Eddy,' I whispered. 'A bloody army of them,'
I continued, vastly exaggerating their numbers. After all, even
ten unexpected enemy soldiers did seem a lot at first glance.
Seven of them moved towards the farm buildings, the other
three and the driver turned in the direction of the barn, and
were lost to view below. We then heard voices. They had
entered the barn.

We dived back into the hay and dug our way in as deeply as
possible, trying to leave a small air passage, as we did so. The
ladder leading up to the loft was still in position, and I

remember cursing myself for not pulling it up into the loft when we had first entered the previous night. I fancied I heard a dog whimper and this was followed by a short sharp bark. Then we sensed, rather than heard, someone climbing the ladder, and soon were conscious of someone poking around in the hay, probably with a pitch fork. We had burrowed deep enough into the hay to avoid being speared and the prodding seemed to be a half-hearted affair anyway. Then a voice spoke, in French.

'*Il n'y-a personne ici.*' We took this to be the voice of the farmer, who must have joined the Germans entering the barn. Who or what they were looking for we had no idea, and never discovered. Had the pitchfork operation continued for any length of time, with possible disastrous results, we would have been left with the choice of giving ourselves up, or lying doggo and receiving serious injury.

Fortunately we didn't have to make this choice, because after one or two more prods, all movement ceased and we heard the conversation become fainter as the person descended the ladder.

We could still hear voices below us and imagined the soldiers perhaps hanging up their equipment and settling down to rest, or even stay permanently, using the barn as a guard post for some unknown reason. In a while the voices ceased and there was silence. Emerging from the hay we discussed the idea of making a break from the farm, for there was no sign of the soldiers, although the lorry was still there. It would be foolish to move until it had gone. We returned to the hay which was warm and cosy and this, combined with the musty sweet smell, caused me to doze off again. Eddy apparently didn't sleep again, and nudged me awake at two o'clock. We looked out of the loop-hole in the roof and saw the Germans climbing back into the lorry with much clattering of equipment and raucous chatter. The lorry started up and emitting clouds of black smoke moved off. The French farmer watched it go, and returned to the barn. We heard him moving around below, then the barn door was closed and there was silence.

We again debated the situation, trying to decide whether to approach the farmhouse and ask for help. At length, we agreed that after the previous evening's escapade, and the recent visit of the German patrol, there was too much German activity in the area, and to put considerable distance between us and the vicinity of Brabant-le-Roi, would be very much to our benefit.

We climbed out of the hay and tried shaking out the chaff from our hair and clothes and after another precautionary glance out through the roof, descended the ladder into the barn below. Approaching the door we found it firmly fastened, from the outside, probably with a heavy bar in sockets. We were well and truly locked in. Exploration failed to find any other exit, and there were no windows. Being strongly built of stone, it would resist anything short of a tank to break out. There remained, therefore, the roof of the loft with the loose tiles I had previously prised away, so up the ladder we went again to the loft, and succeeded in removing sufficient tiles to allow for our exit on to the steeply sloping roof. The farmyard area was completely deserted and although the drop to ground level was fairly formidable, we made it without accident, and set off across open pasture land to the cover of a small copse. Here we ate from the remaining food supplied by the curé the day before and tried to rid ourselves of the hay and chaff. Looking at Eddy, I realised we were a pretty rough, dirty, unshaven couple, cut and scratched, our clothing ripped and torn.

It was now once again approaching evening, the December darkness was fast descending, and we were virtually once again, on our own, as we had been before we arrived in the village of Levoncourt and met Fernand. Up to now we had been lucky to receive the assistance given by him, his family and the curé at Lavallée. More than lucky to have escaped from the supposed 'safe house' in Brabant without capture or injury. So, what now? At least we had companionship in one another, unlike the desperate loneliness I had felt after abandoning the aircraft. We could discuss plans, argue and share confidences. Confidence, that was the important word, the word one was taught in the Service. The confidence a man had in his friends and companions; the confidence a man had in himself. If we lost confidence, I argued, then the physical discomforts of our situation, which were the enemies of confidence, could easily undermine our efforts if we allowed them to take control. Only for a very brief moment did I let the present sense of frustration and uncertainty cloud my outlook. We had to get to Paris, as the curé had told us where we would be sure to get some help to enable us to journey south to neutral Spain. It was a daunting prospect.

'We'd better get cracking again,' I said to Eddy at last. 'Got any ideas?'

'None at all,' he answered, 'except that we continue heading west towards Paris and hope for something to turn up.' Shades of Mr Micawber, I thought.

So we set off across fields, through hedges, and small woods, often stumbling over uneven ground and tripping over broken fence wire, unseen in the gathering darkness. Ground mist began to gather in patches and the stars were not so bright, so that we became apprehensive lest the weather should change and make life more difficult. Now and again, we heard the sound of vehicular traffic from a road somewhere on our right, assuming this to be the main road from Bar-le-Duc towards Revigny, Vitry-le-François and Paris according to our map.

Due to the nature of the terrain, and darkness, we didn't cover much ground that evening and night, and round about three o'clock in the morning we stopped for a rest and another meagre bite from our rapidly depleting food supply. I found myself limping a little, due I surmised, from the jolt I had received in my left leg when I landed in the forest, but a short rest seemed to allay the discomfort. The ground was becoming frost-covered and it was only when we stopped for the rest, that we realised how cold it was and lost very little time getting started again.

Quite suddenly, I heard Eddy swear loudly and collided into his back. He had found himself lurching against some living object in front of him, which turned out to be a cow. The cow never uttered a sound as we pushed past it.

Then we heard a dog bark.

'Where there's a dog, there's a house,' I remarked. 'I vote we make for it, and take a chance on what kind of reception we get. If we carry on out here, much longer, we'll freeze to death or die from exposure.'

'OK,' replied Eddy, 'I'm with you.' We walked in the direction of the barking dog.

The house stood on a slight rise a short distance from a wood; stone built and unattractive. The dog continued barking furiously but we couldn't see it. I led the way and paused momentarily at the gate at the front garden, wondering, even then, whether we were doing the right thing.

'*Qui va là?*'

The voice came from a first floor window.

This was it. No hesitation or change of mind now.

'*Anglais,*' I said. '*Deux aviateurs anglais.*'

'*Attendez,*' and the window closed abruptly.

We waited by the gate, wondering what the outcome would be. There came the rattling of a bolt and the door opened quickly, and an elderly Frenchman stepped out and beckoned us to come forward and enter. We heard the door being bolted behind us. We were in a living room cum kitchen. A lamp, turned down low, was on a table in the centre; on the right stairs led upward and beyond the table was another door. We stood blinking in the light, after the darkness outside. There was a movement overhead, and someone came down the stairs. The elderly Frenchman who had admitted us stood looking at us intently with little bright eyes.

'*Vous parlez français?*'

'*Pas beaucoup,*' replied Eddy.

'*Vous êtes avec amis. N'ayez pas peur.*'

Good, I thought. He seemed genuine.

'*Moi ...*' He pointed to himself, '*soldat aussi. Verdun 1916. Comprenez?*'

'*Oui, oui,*' said Eddy. 'Good show,' he added lamely.

The Frenchman turned towards the stairs where now stood a little elderly woman, with dark wavy hair. She was obviously very nervous and agitated.

'*Ah, Maman,*' the Frenchman cried. '*Voila! Deux aviateurs anglais.*'

The woman's anxiety was not improved by this news because she began wringing her hands and muttering to herself. The Frenchman spoke to her again in rapid French and she immediately busied herself at the kitchen stove. Soon there was a meal of hot soup and bread followed by coffee and cognac and as we ate and drank we gave an account of ourselves arriving in Brabant-le-roi and subsequent lucky escape. We would be on our way just as soon as we could so as not to put him and his wife in any further danger. But the Frenchman would have none of it, and said we would rest here for the remainder of that day, at least and led us into an adjoining room containing a large double bed. Neither of us realised how tired we were until we saw that bed and taking off our outer clothing climbed in and fell asleep almost instantly.

We were awakened in the afternoon having slept for nearly nine hours, by the Frenchman coming in with a jug of coffee. We would again stay in his house that evening and night, but it would be wise not to stay any longer during the day. The Germans were in force in an adjoining village two or three miles distant and very often visited the farm, for milk and eggs. He would therefore conduct us to a neighbouring wood where we would hide and rest until he could think of some way to help us to a further safe abode.

It was early next morning, before sunrise when we left the house for the nearby wood where he left us, saying that his son would come later to see us.

At noon the old man's son, Edmond, he said his name was, brought bread and cheese and milk. With the help of a dictionary which he had brought with him, we were able to converse. The Germans had taken over the school in the village putting an end to his lessons. This, however, allowed him to work more on the farm, and he preferred working outdoors in the fields and with animals. The Germans didn't trouble them much, he said only when they wanted milk and eggs and their general behaviour was reasonable.

After Edmond left in the early afternoon, we dozed and talked, until just before dark, the Frenchman arrived, bringing with him a larger scale map than we already possessed and a further supply of bread and cheese.

We stood together with the little Frenchman at the edge of the wood while he explained the difficulties ahead.

'To the west lies a large forest and a main road being used intensively by the Germans runs through it. Beyond lies a railway line and beyond that a small river. Take care crossing the road and railway that you are not observed and if you keep to the direction you have chosen, you will need to swim the river, since no convenient bridge exists. You would need to contour a great distance north or south to find a crossing. Remember, also, that curfew is from eleven o'clock at night to five in the morning. Anyone seen abroad during those hours is liable to be shot on sight. *Alors – au revoir, et bon voyage.*'

After dark that night we left the wood to begin the next stage of our journey and entered the forest and keeping as straight a course as possible through the trees eventually reached the fringe and were able to see the road running through a narrow cutting. Traffic was indeed heavy and consisted of many types of vehicles, lorries, occasional light tanks, cyclist infantry and motor cycle combinations. They seemed never ending. We watched in the half light for an opening in the stream of traffic, but it was not until after two hours that we risked a quick dash across the road and into the shelter of the trees on the other side of the cutting. The next obstacle was the railway and this proved no bother at all. Judging by the state of the rails, very few trains used it anyway.

Beyond the country was undulating and alternated between cultivated fields, pasture land, small copses and woods. All the time we would still hear, over to our right, the sound of motor vehicles. More than once we were tempted to try and locate the road, which, we argued, would cross our next obstacle, the river. But the volume of traffic which seemed to be using it put us off this idea. It was not worth taking such a chance and we pressed on through the fields.

Dawn was coming up by now and soon daylight filtered through a misty atmosphere and we were sure we were near the river. We could smell the air, somewhat tainted with the musty odour of muddy water and slime. It was unmistakable. We climbed a fence and entered into the short stubble of a cornfield on the other side of which lay a small cluster of buildings. We approached carefully and noted that it consisted mainly of scattered farm buildings with one or two adjacent cottages. Studying the place from the shelter of a low hedge for a matter of just over an hour, we nibbled at some of our remaining bread and cheese and came to the conclusion that the place was deserted. There was no sign of movement, animals or humans and no smoke coming from the cottage chimneys.

We left the shelter of the hedge and reached the farm yard. A gate swung idly on its hinges, whilst just inside was a small barn and a cowshed. A row of hen-houses adjoined the barn, and beyond them was the farm house. Further examination showed that the roof of the house had one or two gaping holes in the slate roof whilst the rear part was completely ruined. One of the cottages was also severely damaged, the walls showing large and small pock marks. It looked as though the place had suffered shell fire or bombing. The nesting boxes in the hen houses contained nothing in the way of eggs or poultry. The whole place looked to have been deserted for a very long time.

The barn contained a ladder tilted up to an open hatch into a loft which, on investigation, contained much straw plus a good number of rats and mice, an ideal resting place had it not been for the rodent population.

Eddy had meanwhile investigated the house, via the front door which stood wide open. There was the customary kitchen living-room, containing a wooden table with only three legs, two wooden chairs and a rocking chair. Climbing the stairs we found three bedrooms each with a bed, without bedding, and covered in dust, plaster and broken tiles from the holes in the roof. A dirt road led up to the house from the right and presumably joined the main road from which we could hear the traffic movements. Exploration of the cottages showed a similar state of affairs although one contained two upholstered armchairs, covered in dust, of course, and the remains of some flowered curtains in one window.

We decided that we would rest a while here during the day before attempting the river crossing that night. In the yard was a pump, which fortunately worked, and a bucket nearby. Filling the bucket with water we put in one or two water-purifying tablets from my escape pack contents, and took it back to the cottage containing the chairs, where we finished off the remaining bread and cheese and settled down to await nightfall.

We left the farm in the late evening under a rising moon, following a path from the rear of the house which led across a field of pasture and once again into a dense wood. It was quite eerie, I remember, in that wood, the noise of traffic from the road subdued by the trees around us. Occasionally we heard movement in the undergrowth and assumed that we were again in the company of wild boar. The track twisted and turned taking all manner of directions but nevertheless, generally heading in the westerly direction where we would find the river. In an hour or so we stepped out of the trees and a few yards ahead the moonlight glinted on the water and we moved forward to the river bank. For a long time, we scouted along the bank in both directions hoping to find a bridge or suitable place to cross without getting wet but our searching proved fruitless. The Frenchman had been right when he said bridges did not exist, and we still did not relish using the main road bridge laden with hostile traffic, as it probably was. We were left with the only other alternative – to swim across. During our scouting along the bank in semi-darkness, we noticed the bank on the far side was, in places, two or three feet high, with over-hanging bushes and trees, and there was no evidence of untoward activity in the vicinity. We were soon to be proved wrong.

We chose a point where the bank seemed less steep and somewhat lower, and undressed. We wrapped our clothing in the black jacket-smocks and knotted the arms around our necks and slipped into the water. God, it was cold, icy cold and I immediately felt a numbness in my lower body. I vigorously trod water to prevent total loss of feeling, then set off, using the breast stroke, partly for quietness and partly to prevent the bundle of clothes getting too wet.

The width at this point must only have been about sixty to seventy feet, I reckoned, but we were deceived by the strength of the current, which being unexpectedly strong carried us across diagonally and we became separated.

It was now very, very dark, and as I approached the high bank and overhang, I was unable to see the top level, or what lay beyond. As I grasped the first overhanging branch, I heard voices above me. I froze and listened. Hell! they were speaking German! This area must be crawling with Germans, I thought. But what were they doing on the river bank? I couldn't see Eddy at all, he must have been a few yards away and I wondered if he had also heard the voices.

My first thought was to turn and swim back to the other bank, but although I must have made some noise as I approached this point, the very fact that now I was aware of hostile presence, made me fear that if I started back, I would immediately be heard, if not seen. Better stay put, and hope it was only a temporary setback.

I sidled carefully along in the water under the overhanging growth trying to find a spot further from the voices, where it would be possible to pull myself out of the water – but it was no use. The bank was so high and steep, I would probably have made too much noise, attempting the scramble, possibly falling back into the water with consequent splashing. No, strangely enough, the only practical place was from where these voices were emanating.

The lower part of my body was intensely cold, being immersed up to chest level, and I kept my legs moving, treading water quietly, in an effort to keep my circulation going. My head and shoulders, although not so chilled, were cold enough. Again I wondered where the hell Eddy was.

Very soon I realised that, come what may, I had to get out of the river or freeze to death. Even now, I contemplated the effect this immersion was going to have, when I did finally get out.

It was gradually getting lighter, and it dawned on me that it was the moon rising, and it was nearly full moon period. In an hour or so the area was bathed in bright moonlight and I decided to risk a peep over the bank edge to see what the situation was. I was able to see that a narrow path ran along the river bank, and at this point there was a sort of small clearing, at the back of which there were some low bushes, and, immediately behind them, a high wire fence with outward pointing supports at the top, crowned with what appeared to be barbed wire. My first conjecture was of a prison compound. Then I thought, the top barbed wire section would have been pointing inwards, if that were the case. This fence was to prevent entry rather than exit. Just off the path, nearer the fence than the river, were two German soldiers, both sitting side by side on a small pile of cut timber. They were not conversing now, and one was puffing a pipe.

At that moment, things began to happen at some speed.

It so happened that just as I had decided to take a peek, the non-smoking soldier shouldered his rifle by the sling, made a short remark to his companion, walked away along the path, and disappeared into the shadows of the riverside trees. I was desperate. I had no intention of sliding back into the river. I had to risk everything, now and with no hesitation. How I wished Eddy was on hand also, as I quickly pulled myself up the bank, trod only four or five quiet steps, barefooted of course, towards the German seated on the log with his back to me. Whether the moon had cast my moving shadow or whether he heard my last footfall, remains unsolved. He reached for his rifle on the timber beside him, and began to turn as I reached and grabbed his helmet, forcibly pulled it backwards over his head, until the strap was round his throat, then twisted the helmet, thereby tightening the strap. He gave a hardly audible gurgle, the rifle slipped from his fingers and he fell backwards at my feet.

Precisely at that moment, either his companion or another German appeared from the trees, where the previous one had disappeared. I think the scene that confronted him must have paralysed him temporarily. He saw a completely naked man, bending over a dead or unconscious soldier in the bright moonlight. An unnerving experience for the strongest of men, I would have thought. For perhaps two seconds, he stood transfixed, certainly no more, and then frenziedly grabbed at his slung rifle. Then the unexpected happened. As I gazed at him, knowing full well that my number was up, out of the corner of my eye, another naked figure appeared out of the river, behind him. In spite of the stark unreality of the situation the most peculiar thought flashed through my mind. As he climbed silently out of the river, I thought, why is he still wearing his underpants? Surely an extreme example of the workings of the human mind, in unexpected or desperate situations.

The German heard him, but was too late to prevent Eddy cannoning into him from behind causing him to fall flat on his face. I do not know what else Eddy did, but the soldier lay motionless face down, as the navigator joined me and we made a hasty departure along the path and into the trees and undergrowth. We ran and stumbled breathlessly and without speaking for a long time, eventually coming out of the rough on to level ground where there were occasional stunted trees and a great many pools. Moss and soaking vegetation, sodden and clammy, were beneath our feet and water oozed between our bare toes.

We decided it was safe to stop and dress again, except for our shoes and socks which we left off due to the nature of the ground. A short way ahead was another railway embankment.

Whether the Germans whom we had left behind were dead or alive, we never found out. Nor did we ever find out what the fence protected. The Germans were without doubt on security duty to whatever lay behind the barbed wire.

We pressed on across the marshy area, and scrambled up the embankment and crossed what turned out to be a single track railway line. Reference to our compass indicated the river and railway running north-south, so we were now again heading westwards. Soon we were approaching a road, also running north-south and noted to the right, the spire of a church. To the left we observed that the road appeared to bend round to a westerly direction so we set off again, took to fields and pastureland to skirt another larger village and found ourselves in very undulating country, so undulating it could almost be called hilly, and we found it hard going for a while. Another village appeared and, putting on our socks and shoes, risked the road for a short distance and found it to be called Vroil, more of a hamlet than a village. The open countryside to the immediate west looked very inhospitable and already we were feeling somewhat tired so we continued to follow the road south which led into a village called Rancourt-sur-Ornain.

As we walked, we fell to discussing whether or not we should take a chance and call into some house, or café, if there was one, and ask for help. It was daylight now so we decided to find a spot where we could study the village for a while and assess the possibilities before attempting to contact anyone. The road now passed over a bridge, spanning a canal, and carried on into the village which lay about four or five hundred yards beyond. We moved off the road up a slight slope on the left where there was a small copse. Choosing a spot among the trees from which we could see most of the village we watched and waited, nibbling at one or two biscuits, some of my precious chocolate and eating an apple from the supply given us by the curé at Lavallée.

The village, like many others, consisted of a straggling line of houses along the main road and one to two little offshoots here and there. There was an air of quiet solitude almost as though the place was deserted and during the couple of hours while we watched, we didn't see any sign of life, apart from a cat which emerged from somewhere, and walked slowly along the road towards the canal bridge. Of course it was still early morning and it was natural that the village was not yet awake.

It was jolly cold sitting around, but we were convinced it was the safest thing to do. The sun was rising and casting a cold wintry light over the village and the surrounding countryside and first signs of life appeared. A farmworker cycled down the road over the canal bridge and disappeared round a road bend.

He was followed, after an interval, by another farmworker, walking behind a dozen cows. From the direction of the canal came another figure on a bicycle and carrying a canvas bag. It was a postman and he carried on up the village street on foot delivering the letters and packages. Overhead came the sound of aircraft engines and two Me109s passed over, heading south-west.

We decided to move and rejoined the road, walking at a steady pace through the village, and we were passing a large building on the right, which was actually the Mairie, when I became conscious of someone slightly behind and keeping pace with us, trying to catch us up and puffing very hard. Between puffs he was trying to speak. I glanced round and saw a tubby man, no more than four foot six tall, with a round moon-like face, rosy cheeks and a wide grin. He also wore large black rimmed spectacles, and it struck me forcibly that he was the image of Billy Bunter but wearing a navy blue beret instead of a Greyfriars school cap. He was having intense difficulty trying to keep up with us and speak at the same time, between breaths. I nudged Eddy's arm, indicated to him the little man trotting along behind me and we slowed our pace.

'Hang on, Eddy,' I said. 'Let's see what this bloke has to say.'

We stopped, and the little man took a deep gulp of air and spoke.

'*Qui êtes vous?*' he demanded breathlessly, looking at us, still wearing his wide cheerful grin. '*Vous êtes anglais,*' he continued. Neither of us answered immediately but looked quickly up and down the road and noted there wasn't another soul in sight.

'*Vous êtes anglais,*' the little man repeated. '*Je suis un ami,*' and grabbing my arm, continued, 'You are airmen. You have been shot down, yes?'

Eddy replied in his best French:

'Yes. We were shot down a few days ago in the Bar-le-Duc area, and were directed to Brabant-le-Roi.'

His grin got wider.

'You stayed in Brabant last night?'

'No,' I answered. 'There was some trouble.'

He didn't press that point, but asked if we were hungry and where we were heading for.

We couldn't answer the second question since we hardly knew ourselves, so I said:

'Thank you, we are not hungry and we have a little food left,' indicating the small knapsack given us by the curé. 'We are thirsty, however, and would welcome a drink.'

There was no doubting his friendliness and sincerity and we had no idea where he had appeared from, as we were marching through the village. We left the next move to him, and waited.

'*Écoutez*!' he exclaimed. 'In the village there is a family who have a young daughter, and she is able to speak English. Continue walking out of the village. About half a kilometre beyond, the road crosses a small stream by means of a low walled bridge.' He puffed a little, as though still out of breath. 'Stop on the bridge,' he continued, 'rest on the parapet and appear to be interested in the stream below. In the meantime, I will go to the house of the girl and tell her about you. She will then come to the bridge and talk to you.'

All this was spoken in French, and pretty rapidly too, but we got the gist of it.

As he finished talking, I saw a cyclist approaching, wearing the uniform of a Gendarme. As he drew level, the little man greeted him in the usual French fashion. The Gendarme dismounted, returned the greeting with a handshake, looked curiously at us and said politely,

'*Messieurs*!', gave us each a brief handshake and turned again to the tubby man who exchanged a few quick words with him, another handshake and the Gendarme mounted his cycle and continued down the road. Whether the Gendarme's suspicions had been aroused at our appearance, or whether our tubby friend had put him in the picture, I know not, but that was the end of the incident anyway.

'*Alors*,' said the tubby man, '*Allez maintenant, et au revoir*,' and moved off the road and disappeared between the houses.

We carried on walking along the road and soon left the village behind. The bridge over the stream was there as he had described, the road continuing beyond, bordered by tall trees. We stopped and waited. We still hadn't seen anyone else and there was no road traffic.

After about twenty minutes, during which time we kept glancing back towards the village, we saw two persons leaving the village on bicycles and begin pedalling up the road. They stopped on the little bridge and dismounted. The man was tall and dark, well built and had a small moustache. The girl was young, about seventeen we judged, and very attractive, with dark hair and grey-blue eyes. They were both dressed in country type clothes. The girl spoke.

'*Bonjour, mes amis,*' she said with a smile. '*Vous êtes anglais, je crois, abbatus près de Bar-le-Duc?*'

'*Bonjour, Mademoiselle,*' we replied together. '*Oui, c'est vrai.*'

'You are lucky,' she remarked. 'There are no Germans in this village, but in Revigny there are many.' Revigny-sur-Ornain was about five kilometres east of Rancourt. 'My name is Odette,' she continued, 'and this is my father,' turning to the man who was now holding the two bicycles. He nodded, smiled, but didn't speak. Odette certainly spoke exceedingly good English. 'Where are you making for?' she asked.

We had to admit that we didn't really know, since after the rumpus at Brabant we weren't sure where we were, and the plan which would have been formulated in the house before the raid was now non-existent due to the appearance of the Germans. Like the little fat man, she didn't press the point about our escape from the house, and neither did she ask the name of the persons or the whereabouts of the house to which we had been directed by Fernand and the curé. We couldn't have told her anyway, since we didn't know any names. I made the point that we didn't know the names of the people in Brabant. She glanced towards her father, and he nodded slowly.

'*Bon. C'est meilleur comme ça.*' That is best!

'What are your names?' enquired Odette.

We told her, and showed our identity tags. She was only interested in our Christian names and I got the distinct impression that they were deliberately avoiding surnames.

Odette spoke again, and almost repeated the advice given us by the curé at Lavallée.

'Your best plan,' she said, 'is to get to Paris as soon as possible. It won't be easy, but if you have money it is worth trying to get there by train. 'Have you money?' she enquired. We agreed we had money. 'When you get to Paris, find your way to 15 Rue St Claude. My uncle lives there, M. Roussel is his name, and he will be able to help you.'

She proceeded to give us directions about how to locate the address, which didn't appear to be too difficult, and emphasized the necessity of memorising what she had told us.

December 28th.

Dear Sir,

I just received a letter from my uncle, Mr Roussel who lives 15 Rue St. Claude in Paris, letter in which your address and Mr Canter's were enclosed. —

You certainly wonder who I am as you Don't know my name but you will perhaps recollect that I gave you Mr Roussel's address on one day when I met you and Mr Canter on the road in France .. My uncle is always very busy and had never before found the time to send me your address; but he had let me know long ago that you and Mr Canter were safe in England. — I had been fretting a lot about your journey and when I heard about you and that everything was all right.

Odette's letter to me after the war. The first page.

From the carriers of the two bicycles, she took two bundles, which, she said contained civilian trousers and socks, a couple of wool scarves, a small quantity of food and a bottle of wine. She and her father then wished us luck, shook hands, mounted their bicycles and pedalled back to the village.

We each took a long drink from the bottle of wine and set off in the opposite direction.

That episode, on a virtually unknown road, outside the village of Rancourt in occupied France, lasted, at the most, ten minutes, but led to a very sincere friendship after the Liberation. Odette obtained our full names and addresses from her uncle and after the war, in 1946, wrote me a very touching letter, telling me how worried and concerned she had been after our parting in 1942, wondering whether we had made a safe journey to England. After the Liberation, she had been happy to receive from her uncle the news that we had successfully made the journey home to England.

Having now orientated ourselves, with Odette's help, we knew the road we were on continued almost due west, and our spirits were considerably raised by the fact that, although somewhat distant, we now had an object in view, the address in Paris. Suddenly, Paris didn't seem to be so far away anymore, but sober thinking reminded us that it was all of 150 or 160 kilometres distant. We began thinking and discussing the possibilities of using the railway. Why not? We had money, probably more than sufficient for the fare, the only danger, and a real one at that, was the absence of proper identity papers. A work permit and ration card which we both had, however authentic, would probably not be entirely satisfactory if we were stopped by German soldiers or police. It was a thought, nevertheless and the nearest main line station, according to our maps, was Vitry-le-François some thirty-odd kilometres distant.

We pressed on, occasionally having to deviate off the road to avoid motorised traffic in each direction. During one of these deviations we changed our uniform trousers for the civilian ones, given us by Odette, leaving the uniform ones hidden in the undergrowth of the woodland. The civilian slacks were a good enough fit, but would not be as warm as the woollen battle-dress ones, and it was decidedly cold. It was late afternoon and the light was beginning to fade, it would soon be dark.

Suddenly we heard the sound of motor vehicle engines coming from ahead of us and gradually getting louder. The road at this point was very straight for a considerable distance and we were able to see, a long way ahead, what we took to be a motorised convoy. We dived off the road into the cover of the woodland hoping that the driver of the first vehicle had not seen our hurried departure, and concealed ourselves as best we could. As the convoy drew level, it stopped and I thought they must have seen us and were going to investigate. It was not the case, however. The vehicles pulled in close to the verge, drivers got out, soldiers who were occupying some of the trucks climbed out and began lighting cigarettes or relieving themselves by the road side. It would seem to be a planned visit, and, of all places, right opposite our place of concealment. We decided evacuation was the order of the day and with considerable care we moved further into the trees and were not detected. Then we began to walk and scramble through the undergrowth between trees and shrubs, parallel to the road. Fortunately it was now quite gloomy as evening approached, and the more intense darkness in the wood gave good cover to our progress. The convoy was a large one, stretching about three or four hundred yards, we reckoned, and as we eventually bypassed the last vehicle decided to keep to the woods.

After about a further hour of difficult and strenuous walking we came upon a narrow path coming from the left, then bending round to continue through the wood almost parallel to the road, and we took it. It was much easier walking. As in the case of the Forêt de Koers, where I had originally landed, a multitude of narrow offshoots branched to left and right and it was from one of these branch paths that a person unexpectedly emerged, so suddenly that we almost collided. The first thing that we both noticed was that he was wearing similar type clothing to Fernand, but in addition he wore a military style Kepi. By his side was a very small boy who was carrying over his shoulder a yard long implement, which we later found out to be an instrument for measuring the girth of a tree. Another forestry worker, I thought. Are we going to be lucky again? We exchanged the usual greetings, in French and made to continue as the man stared solemnly at us, obviously curious about our accent. He was of middle age, mild-eyed and quite self-possessed and registered no surprise at our sudden appearance. Eddy suddenly said to me, quite settled in his mind how to approach the situation,

'Let's give it a try. The chap seems genuine.'

I nodded. Perhaps the direct method would succeed and anyway we needed somewhere with a roof and warmth for a night's rest. We had food previously given us by Odette, but as an opening preamble, I said, in French:

'Can you give us some food, please?'

The man continued to stare, curiosity written all over his face.

'*Vous n'êtes pas francais,*' he replied. 'Who are you?'

'We are English,' Eddy said. 'RAF shot down,' he continued.

'*Alors.*' The forester turned. 'Follow me.'

We followed. The little boy trotted along between us chattering away in French which we hadn't the remotest chance of understanding.

Presently the path emerged from the trees and entered the environs of a farm and, passing a cow byre and pigsty, the lights of the farmhouse appeared through the darkness. The boy ran ahead and pushed open the door and we followed the Frenchman into the house.

There was a man and a woman seated at the kitchen table as we came in. Our escort again spoke, this time addressing himself to us.

'How far have you come?' he asked.

Having decided to take these people into our confidence, we related the whole series of events since we baled out, referring only to the Christian names of the people who had helped us. The explanation was accepted with blank stares by all three, except when we mentioned Odette's name, when a flicker of interest showed in the woman's eyes and she looked at the two Frenchmen, who nodded understandingly and returned their gaze to us.

'So you are making for Paris?' said the man sitting at the table. 'It is many kilometres to walk, and not without danger.' He turned and spoke to the woman, and I heard Odette's name mentioned. We replied that we understood this and, according to Odette's suggestion, it seemed the logical thing to do, and in any case had we any alternative?

The two men consulted together in rapid French,

occasionally addressing their remarks to the woman who seemed to share their views. Our escort spoke.

'*Bon! Ça va bien!* You will eat here with us this evening, and you will sleep here overnight. We have room for you. Tomorrow morning you will arise early. You will be accompanied to the railway station and board the train for Paris.'

How strange, I thought. It was just that afternoon that we had been discussing that very possibility, and here it was, being laid on for us. We showed our enthusiasm for the proposition also voicing our anxiety over the question of identity papers, should the eventuality arise. On this point, we were told that it was a risk we would have to accept, and we resigned ourselves to this fact.

We dined and wined, that evening, simply but well, and were more than ready for bed when we were led upstairs and ushered into a large bedroom containing a double bed. Bidding our host goodnight, we gratefully tumbled into the bed and after a brief debate about the possible outcome of the morrow's events, slept soundly.

CHAPTER SIX

Next Stop Paris

We were awakened shortly after six o'clock in the morning by
Madame entering with a basin of water for washing, and what
seemed the miracle of all miracles, a razor to shave, between us.
Using the small tablet of ersatz washing soap, we managed a
sketchy and rather painful shave, and felt much better for it.
We breakfasted off coffee and bread rolls and whilst eating,
were instructed on our coming journey.

We would be forestry workmen, carry the necessary tools of
our trade, Eddy, a large double-handed saw, and I, the
instrument that the little boy had carried the night before for
measuring tree-girth. We would ride bicycles to the railway
station at Vitry-le-François. We would be accompanied by the
man who had been in the house when we arrived but on the
train we would occupy one compartment and he would travel
separately and rejoin us at the Gare de l'Est in Paris. We must
avoid conversation with anyone, but if we were spoken to, we
should use a very guttural voice and just say 'Breton'.
Fortunately there were still people in Brittany who did not
speak ordinary French. Finally, the person who would be our
escort was well associated with the conductor of the particular
train on which we would travel. If German police boarded the
train at either of the two stops before Paris, Chalôns-sur-
Marne or Château-Thierry, this conductor would warn our
escort who, in turn would warn us, and then it may be necessary
to abandon the train, risking the chance of injury in the
process. Not very reassuring! Soon it was time to leave and
fastening our woodman's tools to the bicycles provided for us,
we said our goodbyes, voiced our thanks to the couple whose
hospitality we had enjoyed, mounted the bicycles and together
with our escort set out for the station.

At this juncture, it might be noted that not one name had

90

ever been mentioned since our arrival. We never did find out who these people were, but after the war during a visit to Odette, at Rancourt, I learned that a Frenchman answering to the description I gave, had been arrested, cruelly interrogated, eventually shot for subversive activities and his wife and son deported to Germany. I prefer to think that these brave people did not suffer solely on our account since I cannot imagine how the Germans would have known of the personal help they gave us. No doubt, further clandestine activities after our departure, which might have included assisting other shot-down flyers to escape, but also probably included sabotage and general resistance to the occupation, were contributory reasons for their arrest and subsequent harsh treatment.

We learned, however, that our escort called himself Bernard and he told us that it would be about one and a half to two hours ride to the station using country back roads, rather than the main road so as to avoid any early morning traffic, military or otherwise. It was only half light when we started off, but after half an hour or so it was nearly daylight, the sun slowly rising behind us, and glistening on the frosty branches of the trees bordering the road. Although it was very cold, steady pedalling kept the circulation going and the ride could have been a pleasant experience had it been in more normal circumstances. As it was, we were thinking more of the hazards of the coming train journey to Paris, plus the concentration of riding on the right of the road, rather than the beauty of a frosty morning's cycle ride.

The journey passed without incident and we arrived at the station where Bernard told us to wait outside whilst he purchased the tickets with the money we had given him. I saw him pause and have a few words with someone in uniform, whom I took to be the station master and I reflected that perhaps he was ascertaining for certain that the train conductor would be the associate who would give warning of the police joining the train en route. There were one or two people waiting around and strolling about, mostly country types carrying baskets and small bundles. Suddenly a German military lorry roared into the station yard and disgorged about twenty soldiers, in charge of an NCO who marched them past us into the station. The lorry turned smartly about, and disappeared quickly away, in the direction it had come.

Bernard returned with the train tickets and leaving the bikes against the wall, we entered the station carrying our woodman's tools, trying to look as inconspicuous as possible. Actually I am firmly convinced that we need not have tried, because in our borrowed attire I'm certain we looked no different from any others of the local population. There were more uniformed Germans on the platform than French civilians, and it was a somewhat unnerving feeling, practically rubbing shoulders with enemy soldiers and I wondered what their reaction would have been if they were later to be told that the two Frenchmen they had seen on Vitry-le-François station platform, carrying woodman's implements were really English airmen. The mind boggles!

Soon the train arrived and our escort motioned us into a compartment already almost full of civilian travellers; he himself entered a compartment further to the rear of the train. The journey to Paris took just over two hours and passed without incident, no German control, no French police check only a ticket inspection by the train conductor. One Frenchman in the compartment tried to make conversation but soon gave it up, when all he received in reply were unhelpful grunts.

The train pulled into the Gare de l'Est, Paris about one o'clock. For a full half hour before that, the occupants of the compartment began to make themselves ready for a quick exit, pulling down bundles and cases from the roof racks, slinging them on to their shoulders or resting them on their knees. Everyone had that look of anticipation on their face which spelled that he or she was determined to be the first out, on arrival, the only doubt being that no one knew which side of the train would be the exit point. Nevertheless they braced themselves for the plunge and it was clear that there would be no trace of delicacy or politeness when the time came, it would be every man for himself. We sat back, unmoved and quite content to be last in the queue. As soon as the train entered the station, everyone stood up and made for the door into the corridor, and that was as far as they got, since everyone else in other compartments had the same ambition and were doing similarly, resulting in the corridor itself becoming blocked with humanity and luggage. Eventually all the occupants of our compartment managed to lever themselves out of the narrow door, voicing apologies as they pushed and trod on one

Author's route through France.

another's toes in this seemingly desperate effort to exit. We remained seated watching this amazing performance, then deciding it would be beneficial to keep within the crowd when going through the barrier, descended on to the platform and joined the crowd.

Approaching the barrier I saw our escort a short way ahead and giving no sign of recognition until we also were safely through. Although there were armed German soldiers at the barrier in addition to the ticket collectors, there was no demand for papers and we passed through into the main concourse and towards the exits to the streets of the city.

Out of the station there was a sobering sense of relief, and from nowhere our escort appeared and led us along a busy pavement and across the road into the wide Boulevard Magenta which led presently into the Place de la République, across which we entered the Boulevard du Temple and continued into Boulevard Beaumarchais. It was quite a long walk and there were many in German uniform walking or sitting in the various cafés and brasseries lining the boulevards. Some were smart, others somewhat untidy and many looking to be out of their element in this fashionable city. The Parisiens themselves, particularly the women, carried themselves well, and in spite of everything obviously were trying to keep to their reputation of dressing smartly, and made no attempt to conceal their disdain of the wearers of 'field grey'. Suddenly we turned off the boulevard into a narrow side street on the right. This was Rue St Claude, where lived M. Roussel, the uncle of Odette. It was not a long street and only wide enough to allow one vehicle to pass through comfortably, two could pass by mounting the pavement on each side, and it connected the Boulevard Beaumarchais with the Rue du Turenne. About halfway along was a cul-de-sac on the right with a small café on the corner, opposite which, was number fifteen, the home of M. Roussel. Here our escort bade us goodbye, saying he must catch a train back to Vitry-le-François.

The entrance to number fifteen was a large wide gate with a small opening cut within the larger. Eddy opened the small door and we realised we were in a small covered courtyard. A path led us to another door upon which we knocked. There was no reply. After having knocked a number of times, we retraced our steps to the large gate and emerged into the little street pondering about our next move.

'How about inquiring in that café on the corner?' said Eddy. 'Someone in there might know him and have an idea where he is, and how long he will be. It's worth a chance, we can't wander around Paris for the rest of the day, and possibly all night as well.'

'Yes,' I replied. 'Let's have a go.'

We crossed the narrow street to the door of the café which had net curtains obscuring the view into the interior. Eddy pushed open the door and we entered. A woman was standing behind the bar and three men were leaning on it talking to her. We selected a table near the door away from the bar. Catching the woman's eye, I said:

'Madame, two coffees please.'

'*Oui, Monsieur.*'

The coffee was brought and we sipped it slowly, hoping that the three men might soon leave, when we would tackle the problem alone with the woman behind the bar. Soon two of the men said goodbye and left. The third man remained at the bar. The cafés in occupied France had become clubs for acquaintances and friends. Some were centres for free gossip between well known friends, for passing news of the war and airing hatred of the oppressors. Some, only a very few, were centres for conspiratorial meetings concerning sabotage and resistance. The entry of a stranger would cause immediate suspicion and conversation would dry up just as quickly. The remaining man turned and briefly glanced in our direction before ordering another drink from the woman. We had to make some move, and agreeing, decided this was the moment.

'*Madame,*' I said, '*connaissez vous M. Roussel?*'

At the mention of the name Roussel, the man at the bar abruptly turned and surveyed us with a mixture of curiosity and suspicion. The woman didn't answer, and she also looked fixedly at us. It seemed we had caused something of a hiatus.

I continued, 'We were asked to call and see M. Roussel at his home in Rue St Claude.'

'Who by?' shot the man at the bar, at the same time moving his right hand to the inside of his jacket.

Golly, I thought. He's got a gun!

Eddy thinking likewise, decided to make a clean break of it, to hell with the consequences.

'We met his niece yesterday in Rancourt,' he said quickly, in his best French. 'We are English'. Jointly, we briefly recounted the events of the past two days. The explanation seemed to satisfy both man and woman, particularly when we produced our RAF identity tags. The woman came from behind the bar, and locked the café door, returned to the bar and disappeared through a door at the back. She reappeared with two large cups of coffee and some bread rolls and set them down before us and smilingly told us to eat. The man came across from the bar, sat down at the table and asked us to tell him more. We related our story, after which he told us that the café was the meeting place for a Resistance group working in that quarter of Paris and M. Roussel was one of the organisers. In an hour, other members of the group would be coming to the café for a discussion, he told us. His name was Charles and he was a gendarme. The woman behind the bar, was the café owner, also a member of the group and her name was Bernadette. No secrecy here, I thought, and a gendarme of all people, an active member of a Resistance group! Apparently we had a lot to learn about the operations of this underground warfare into which we had stumbled.

Whilst Charles was talking to us, Madame Bernadette unlocked the door of the café which she had previously locked, during the tense moment when we had enquired about M. Roussel and revealed our identities. She then spoke to Charles in rapid French, and he in turn, turned to us and speaking slowly in French said it would be safer for us to go upstairs to await arrival of his friends. We got up from the table and mounted a narrow flight of stairs, which we hadn't previously noticed in a corner of the café and entered into a large room overlooking Rue St Claude immediately over the downstairs café bar.

Charles followed us and took the precaution of partly drawing the window curtains, told us not to show ourselves at the window and left us, to return downstairs. The room was simply furnished with a long trestle table around which were a number of dining chairs. The floor was uncarpeted. A built-in cupboard occupied one corner, a large heavy sideboard, one wall and a tall empty bookcase the other together with a small electric convector heater. Apart from probably being used as a meeting room, it could also be used, in better times as an overflow from the café below and for party functions.

Left on our own we could only discuss and recap on our

Befehl

Wer Englaender beherbergt,

hat diese bis zum **20. Oktober 1940**

der naechsten Kommandantur

der deutschen Wehrmacht anzumelden.

Wer Englaender nach dieser rist weiterhin beherbergt, hne sie angemeldet zu haben,
WIRD ERSCHOSSEN.

ru, den 13. Oktober 1940.

För den Oberbefehlshaber des Heeres
DER CHEF DER MILITAERVERWALTUNG IN FRANKREICH.

Ordre

Celui qui héberge des Angl

doit en faire la déclaration

pour le **20 Octobre 1940**,

a la Commandantur de l'armée allema

la plus proche.

Celui qui continuera à berger des Anglais après délai, sans les avoir déclar
SERA FUSILLÉ

Paris, le 13 Octobre 1940.

Pour le Commandant en chef de l'arm
LE CHEF DE L'ADMINISTRA MILITAIRE EN FRANCE.

Posters fixed to the walls of towns and villages in France. *Above:* Those who shelter Englishmen must make a declaration by 20 October 1940 to the nearest Army Commander. Those who continue to shelter Englishmen after this period, not having declared them, will be shot. Paris 13 October 1940. *Below:* Any male person directly or indirectly helping the crew of enemy aircraft landed by parachute or having made a forced landing, or assisting them in their evasion, or hiding or helping them in any way whatever will be shot immediately. Women guilty of the same offence will be deported to concentration camps in Germany. Any persons seizing crew members who have forced landed or come down by parachute, or who by their attitude contribute to their capture, will receive a reward of up to 10,000 francs. In some special cases this reward will be even higher. Paris, 22 September 1941.

BEKANNTMACHUNG

Jede mannliche Person, die notgelandete oder durch Fallschirmabsprung gerettete feindliche Flugzeugbesatzung u direkt oder indirekt unterstützt, ihnen zur Flucht verhilft, sie verbirgt oder ihnen sonstwie behilflich ist, wird sofort standrechtlich erschossen.

Frauen, die derartige Unterstützungen leisten, werden in Konzentrationslager nach Deutschland abgeführt.

Personen, die notgelandete Flugzeugbesatzungen oder Fallschirmabspringer sicherstellen, oder durch ihr Verhalten zur Sicherstellung beitragen, erhalten eine Belohnung bis zu 10000 Frs. In besonderen Fällen wird die Belohnung noch erhoht.

Paris, den 22. September 1941.

Der Militärbefehlshaber in Frankreich.
VON STUELPNAGEL
General der Infanterie.

AVIS

Toute personne du sexe masculin qui pu tera une aide directe ou indirecte à des équipag d'avions ennemis forcés d'atterrir ou de de cendre en parachute, qui les aidera à s'enfuir a se cacher, ou qui leur portera une ai quelconque, sera immédiatement passée par l armes.

Toute personne du sexe féminin qui le prêtera une aide analogue sera transférée da un camp de concentration en Allemagne.

Toute personne qui réussira à capturer d équipages d'avions ennemis ou des parachutiste ou qui, par sa conduite, contribuera à assure leur capture, recevra une récompense pouva aller jusqu'à 10.000 Frs. Cette récompens pourra même être augmentée dans certains cas

Paris, le 22 Septembre 1941.

Le Commandant Militaire en France.
VON STUELPNAGEL
Général de l'Infanterie.

Above With Monique Spequel in the rue Perronet, Neuilly, in 1983. This is the same flat in which she hid me for some days in Paris.

Pat O'Leary snapped unawares by a street photographer in Marseille. *(Courtesy of Vincent Brome)*

Certificate issued to me after successfully crossing the Pyrenees into Spain.

Afterwards! Myself about 1948 (*above*), and the annual camp at RAF Waddington, July 1966, while serving with the Volunteer Reserve (*below*).

Right The graves of Pilot Officer Hillier and Sergeant Smith in the cemetery at Courouvre, where the Halifax crashed. The crosses have now been replaced by the Official War Graves headstones.

RAF WADDINGTON OPERATIONS WING

Ceremony at Courouvre in May 1986 at the graves of Pilot Officer Hillier and Sergeant Smith.

Myself at Revigny in May 1986.

unusual lucky breaks of the past seven days, and ponder on what the next move would be in the chain of events. The thought did enter our minds as to whether we were onto something good, or whether we were putting our heads into well greased nooses. Our cards were on the table, face upwards, our progress to date could, with some difficulty, be traced back and – well it was just not worth contemplating.

Soon, we became aware of the murmur of voices from downstairs and the sound of footsteps mounting the stairs. The members of the group, or some of them, had evidently arrived, or was it someone else, less welcome? Our fears proved to be groundless! Three young men entered the room, came straight over and greeted us warmly in turn. The first a tall, slim youth with sleek black hair and brown eyes spoke:

'*Je m'appelle Yves*,' he said, '*et les deux*,' he indicated his companions, '*ils sont mes amis, Mario et Philippe*.' They both nodded in agreement and sat down at the long table.

'*Parlez vous Français?*' Yves demanded.

We replied that we both spoke French very little indeed.

'It does not matter,' said Yves, 'some of us speak a little English also. You have been sent to meet M. Roussel, I believe? You met his niece in Rancourt?'

'Yes,' I replied, 'she was very helpful and very kind.' At this moment, more voices were heard downstairs and more feet began ascending the stairs. Five more men entered, two of whom were the men who had been talking to Bernadette in the café, also Charles, the gendarme. After being introduced they also took their places at table, and soon Madame arrived with the inevitable bottles of wine and tray of glasses. Yves proceeded to ask us what part of England we came from, had we any family, what were conditions really like in England, how were we standing up to German air raids.

He never enquired the number of our squadron, but asked what kind of bomber we had flown in. I was relieved for two reasons. One, we were not supposed to divulge our squadron number, if we were taken prisoner, but we hadn't been informed of what to do regarding giving this information to possible friends. Secondly, I thought, if these people were not what we hoped they were, then they surely would have asked for our squadron number, and where our base was. So we were fairly well convinced that we were in friendly hands. They, in their turn seemed to be confident that we were truly British airmen.

'Have you any plans?' enquired Yves.

'We naturally want to get out of France and back to England. The curé told us the best thing to do was to get to Paris, then to Toulouse and eventually Spain. We have no plan, but hope to reach the border, and walk over the mountains.'

'*Alors*,' replied Yves, 'yes that is the only way, but very difficult you realise. Crossing the Pyrenees anywhere is not easy, and apart from the risk of encountering border patrols there will be a lot of snow at this time of year. However with the mountain guides, it can be done.'

We agreed, but persisted that we could only but try.

'You will remain here this afternoon and evening, perhaps also until tomorrow, while we make all necessary arrangements, M. Roussel will be here soon and he will decide what to do,' said Yves.

It was not long before the sound of footsteps on the stairs heralded the arrival of M. Roussel. He was a slightly rotund man of medium height with a somewhat pale complexion and pale blue intelligent-looking eyes. He wore a long black coat, buttoned high to the neck, and a black beret covered his head. His attire gave him the appearance of a member of the clergy. He greeted us first, effusively and warmly then turned to the rest of the company, greeting them in turn. Taking his place at the table, a discussion was entered into, in voluble French, only odd words and phrases of which we were able to understand, sufficiently enough to know, that we were a major subject of the debate.

The meeting came to a close and Bernadette departed with the wine glasses and bottles remarking that soon we would have dinner. Two of the men excused themselves and departed, presumably on other business whilst the remainder it seemed were to partake of a meal with us. A general conversation developed in which we took part, not without language difficulty and we learned that Yves was some kind of civil servant; three of his companions were school teachers, two others were students, another was a car mechanic, one a railway worker, whilst Charles, as we were already aware, was a gendarme. As regard M. Roussel, his profession or vocation remained a mystery, whether by design or accident, I know not.

We thought it prudent not to enquire.

Madame reappeared soon to prepare the table for the evening meal which turned out to be of gargantuan proportions considering the problems of rationing and shopping. I reckon there was no shortage of money since the food provided could only have been purchased through black market sources. We offered to surrender all the Belgian and French currency we had, but this was refused, politely but firmly. We might find we needed it on some future occasion, she said.

Meantime the café below was attended to by two friends of Bernadette who were employed part-time in the evenings, when business was brisk, many German soldiers, as well as the locals patronising the premises sublimely ignorant of the upstairs activities.

The meal came to an end, and M. Roussel said we would spend the night in Bernadette's flat, which was situated adjacent to the café in the cul-de-sac. Tomorrow some fresh clothing would be found so as to make us more presentable in the city and after the last customer had departed from the café, we trooped down the stairs, said our goodnights to our friends, and were directed to the flat owned by Bernadette.

Here, before turning in, Bernadette told us her late husband had been an army officer killed in the fighting before the collapse of France and she chose to continue running the café, both as a business to occupy her mind and as a clandestine meeting place for M. Roussel, Yves and his friends who were engaged on building a strong resistance group and possibly an escape line to the south. Already two English soldiers left back after Dunkirk, had been passed through the organization, but it was not known how far they had progressed after leaving Paris. We were the first airmen to be encountered.

CHAPTER SEVEN

Strange Hideouts

We were awakened at nine the following morning by Bernadette who told us to wash and dress and come down to her little kitchen where there would be coffee and bread. Yves would arrive later, probably bringing some respectable clothing to change into. We had spent a comfortable night in the little flat and were feeling much less apprehensive of the risks these people were taking due to the fact that they seemed to be fully aware of what they were about, and were taking every precaution. We breakfasted and Yves arrived, accompanied by M. Roussel, and carrying two parcels which contained various articles of clothing including clean underwear. Personally I was loathe to part with the warm RAF issue flying underwear and sweater, but was pacified when M. Roussel said they would be washed and returned to us in a day or two, since we would be remaining in Paris for a few days. The outer clothing fitted us not too badly and included two thick overcoats which were to prove a godsend a few weeks later, whilst soft flat caps completed the ensemble.

We were now to move to another address in the city since it was safer not to stay too long under the same roof, but we would still be in the care of Yves and his friends. The new address was in the south of Paris near Place d'Italie to which we would need to walk, guided by Yves. M. Roussel bade us goodbye and good luck, explaining that he personally may not see us again before we left Paris, but Yves would look after us.

'When we leave the flat,' said Yves, 'follow a few paces behind me and make no attempt to speak to me again until we are indoors. You look quite inconspicuous, no different from anyone else on the streets, so have no fear, but keep me in sight. If we *do* become separated, return immediately to the café and wait there.'

We assented that we understood and off we went, down Boulevard Beaumarchais, across Place de la Bastille over the Seine by the Pont Sully, then by a network of narrow back streets across the Place d'Italie and into a small street between a bank and large restaurant. The street was entirely empty and we saw Yves disappear into a doorway near the far end. Making sure the street was still empty, we followed. Yves was waiting in the little hall where some stairs led upwards. Ascending the stairs we arrived on a small landing, the stairs continuing up to the premises above. Yves pressed a bell push to the right of the door, and it was opened by a middle-aged woman who immediately recognised Yves and then looked expectantly at us. It was evident that she had been previously advised of the visit, expressing no surprise at our appearance and ushered us into the flat. After the usual greeting and a glass of wine, Yves said he must leave, but we would be safe here until his return, then made his departure.

The woman introduced herself as Beatrice, her husband Raoul, was an accountant and his office was nearer the centre of Paris. They owned a car but petrol being so difficult to obtain M. Raoul had to use the Metro to and from his office. They had two daughters both working in Lyon as secretaries, and we would occupy their bedroom while they were absent.

Yves did not return that day, nor did he show up the following day which made us feel a little worried. Beatrice told us not to worry, Yves and his friends had many things to attend to and even now could be making plans on our behalf. So we dismissed our worries as best we could, and enjoyed the comfort and hospitality of Beatrice and her husband.

On Tuesday, Yves arrived in the late afternoon accompanied by Charles, with the news that we had to move again, that evening, to another safe address. No time was wasted and, having said a hurried goodbye to Beatrice, we were on our way once more. It was dusk and street lamps were coming on along the main boulevards. We were led through a network of narrow streets and lanes to the Metro at Corvisant and boarded a train for Montparnasse where we had to change to another line and soon found ourselves at Place Clichy, near Montmartre. Again through a maze of side streets we arrived at a tall block of flats, entered, mounted to the fourth floor by elevator and were welcomed into the flat of an attractive young girl, introduced to us as Germaine.

'You will remain here until Thursday,' Yves said, 'Germaine will give you a meal and leave you until tomorrow. You will be quite safe here, in fact probably safer than anywhere else in Paris. It's a brothel! The place will be crawling with Germans day and night, but the last thing they will be looking for will be RAF escapers.'

Germaine laughed, seemingly enjoying the situation, and our obvious embarrassment and produced a bottle of wine and glasses. Charles and Yves drank swiftly and left.

Germaine could speak pretty good English and told us she had stayed in England for eighteen months, with an aunt, married to an Englishman, who lived and worked near Birmingham. She explained that many of the brothel girls, including herself, were involved with the underground movement now taking shape in Paris and revelled in monstrously overcharging their German clients. Sometimes they were able to glean information which proved useful to the Resistance group. After preparing a cold meal, she sorted out some English books and magazines, showed us where we would sleep, bade us '*bonsoir, dormez bien,*' and left.

In fact, we didn't stay there until Thursday. Yves arrived the following afternoon, told us we were moving again, and left a note for Germaine explaining the situation. Later we were to learn that the prostitutes of Paris, and probably of other large cities in France, were extremely patriotic, and they could be relied upon implicitly to shelter Allied servicemen, feed them and often act as couriers along part of an escape route. It was rumoured that on one occasion a number of girls acting together in some planned operation in the Lyon and Marseilles area, were betrayed, the majority of them being shot. Even this disaster proved insufficient to deter them from the continuation of their activities.

Once more our journey was by the Metro, and, emerging from the station, we found ourselves in the area of Tuileries gardens, flanked by the Rue de Rivoli. A short walk brought us to the entrance of what appeared to be a very high class restaurant.

Opposite the large entrance was a bus stop where one or two people were waiting including a man reading a newspaper, who slowly detached himself from the little queue and preceded us.

It was Charles, our gendarme friend, and it was obviously a pre-arranged meeting. Walking ahead, a distance of about fifty yards, he suddenly turned left into a side street and Yves followed, motioning us to do likewise, and soon caught up with Charles, when a rapid few words were exchanged. We turned sharp left again and I began to realise that we were now at the back of the restaurant.

Charles and Yves led us into the rear entrance, which gave access to the kitchens. Passing along a passage, we arrived at a glass door leading into a large office where sat a well dressed man, smoking a cigarette. He was evidently well acquainted with our escorts because he rose quickly, his expression showing recognition.

'Bonjour, mes amis, et vous aussi,' he said looking at Eddy and me. 'Asseyez-vous un moment.'

A conversation then ensued between himself and our escorts. It seemed that we were to stay at this restaurant, in the owner's flat above the dining-room, and this gentleman, who was the manager, had already been briefed about our arrival by his boss, the restaurateur. The latter person was not, however, immediately available because a very special guest had arrived unexpectedly to whom VIP treatment was being accorded. The special guest turned out to be no lesser person than the German Military Governor of Paris, General von Stülpnagel. I suppose we could be forgiven for the look of astonishment first appearing on our faces, followed by a shadow of anxiety at the thought of being sheltered in the confines of an establishment patronised by high-ranking German officers, and the manager was not slow to notice our discomfort.

'Have no qualms, my friends,' he said cheerily. 'You couldn't be in any other safer place, except perhaps, where you slept last night. Monsieur Roullier, who is the owner of this restaurant, is held in high esteem by von Stülpnagel and his staff and, as a result of the personal attention which he offers them, receives in return many favours. The Germans trust him implicitly.' He laughed. 'On the other hand, his loyalty to France and the Resistance groups of Paris remains unquestionable, and has been proved beyond doubt, so have no fear, *mes amis.*' His obvious sincerity and the replete confidence with which he was imbred very soon put us at ease. After all, a restaurant virtually crawling with Germans would be one of the last places suspected of being a safe hideout for RAF escapers and evaders.

Yves and Charles, after a brief exchange of words with the manager, gave us a reassuring thumbs-up sign and swiftly left, again by the back entrance.

The manager, who said his name was André, then produced a small ring of keys from a drawer, and motioning us to follow, led us from the office up some stairs to the first floor flat, to which, he said, M. Roullier would come as soon as possible, and told us to feel at home and relax.

The flat was extensive with lounge, kitchen-diner and two large bedrooms, and was tastefully furnished with small expensive-looking furniture, a cabinet of china and a large bookcase of finely bound books. In a short while, Robert Roullier arrived and quietly introduced himself. He would be in his middle forties, I reckoned, and was typically French, with dark brown hair, brushed back from a fine high forehead, and a genial compelling and scholarly face. He expressed keen interest in our activities before arriving in Paris and reaffirmed what his manager had told us regarding the safety of the restaurant. Up to the beginning of 1942, he told us, the Germans in Paris, officers and other ranks, had been very assiduous in their relations towards Parisians, politeness and consideration being the order of the day. However a different type of German had become increasingly evident on the streets, dressed in civilian clothes and wearing long raincoats and dark felt hats. These were the dreaded Gestapo and had neither good manners or military smartness. There was no love lost between the Wehrmacht or the Luftwaffe and these newcomers, so consequently the restaurant had not been patronised by them – yet.

'You will remain in this flat for maybe a few days, after which arrangements will have been completed to take you south, where I know facilities exist for you to cross the Pyrenees into Spain. I am sure of this, because it has already been done successfully.'

We spent the next three days confined in the flat and in supreme comfort. We wanted for nothing except perhaps fresh air and outdoor exercise. It was here that I became somewhat out of sorts, the first and the only time I felt unwell during my sojourn in France. Whether it was delayed reaction, or something I had eaten, I do not know, but spent a good proportion of my stay charging back and forth to the toilet, and couldn't face much of the appetising food which was provided for us daily. By the third day I was feeling much better, and was able to enjoy a meal of moderate proportions.

On the 19th, M. Roullier visited us in the evening as he usually did, and we learned from him that we were to leave the following day, by train, to a small town many miles south of Paris and well on the way towards the Spanish frontier. Yves and Charles would accompany us, and since he, himself, would not be available in the morning, wished us luck and a safe journey. To the best of our ability, we expressed profuse thanks for the hospitality, consideration and help given us over the past few days. Our inner feelings regarding the great risk this man was taking remained unspoken, they were beyond expression.

The following morning provided an event which for sheer audacity is difficult to believe. Yves arrived, alone, at nine o'clock, carrying a small case containing the clothing previously left at Rue St Claude for washing. He led us downstairs to the front entrance where, at the kerb, stood a black Citroën saloon car, a uniformed German at the wheel. Yves opened the rear door and, noting not unnaturally, our apprehension and hesitancy, hissed:

'Get in quick!'

We climbed in, the German let in the gear and we moved off.

Apparently, the previous evening von Stülpnagel had again dined at the restaurant and during conversation M. Roullier had mentioned that two friends who had been staying with him were catching a train in the morning and his car had developed some defect which prevented him driving them to the station. Without hesitation the German said he would provide a car and driver to do the job, and true to his word, had done just that.

We soon arrived at the Gare d'Austerlitz where we climbed out of the car and entered the station. At the platform barrier Charles was waiting and gave each of us a train ticket which he had purchased beforehand. The train was already in the platform and passengers were in the process of boarding. We noted that the destination boards of the train read Bordeaux, Dax and Tarbes, and our tickets bore the destination Ruffec. On the advice of Yves, we chose a compartment occupied by a number of French civilians, whilst he and Charles entered a different compartment further along the train.

The journey was uneventful and we were again lucky in that no police check took place, only the usual ticket inspection by the conductor. Very few stops were made, and after Poitiers, Yves appeared in the corridor and indicated that we would alight at the next stop. Ruffec is a pleasant little country market town, situated approximately half way between Poitiers and Angoulême in the department of the Charente, where the river, of the same name, shelters the famous Cognac vineyards. Very few passengers alighted and we mixed with them through the exit from the platform and into the station yard. Near the entrance, I noticed a German military transport truck parked, with two soldiers lounging against the bonnet and smoking. They showed no interest as we passed and soon we were joined by Yves and Charles who led us through the town, until we arrived near the Hôtel de Ville in the market square, where we entered a narrow road by the side of a dental surgery. We would come to know the surgery and the adjoining house very well, since it was to be our safe refuge for quite a while. Answering Yves's knock on a side door we were welcomed into a spacious barnlike structure which, among other things, contained two cars, thence through a further door into a courtyard and garden, which backed on to the surgery. The lady who welcomed our little party was of no great stature, but very robust, fresh-faced and wore a cheerful smile. She would be about forty, I reckoned. She exchanged warm greeting with Yves and Charles with whom she was obviously acquainted and conducted us through French windows into a large dining room, rather sombrely decorated, furnished with heavy antique furniture and cosily warm after coming in from the chill December air.

'This is Madame Denivelle,' said Yves. 'She is a dentist and, together with her husband, Gaston, will look after you until further arrangements can be made.'

'*Bonjour, mes enfants,*' said Madame Denivelle, '*Vous êtes bien venue, ici en Ruffec. Comment allez vous?*'

We returned her greetings, and somehow, speaking for myself, I felt very much at home with her. During the next few weeks her confidence and cheerfulness was an inspiration and helped us to forget the actual danger which still existed.

We sat around a large dining table, where presently the inevitable bottles and glasses appeared, and over the drinks an intensive conversation developed with Yves and Charles, very little of which we were able to understand due to its rapidity.

At the end of the discussion, Yves again told us that Madame Denivelle was a surgeon dentist, the only one in Ruffec and most of her time would be spent in the surgery during the day, but she employed a trustworthy housemaid who cooked and looked after general household duties. Gaston Denivelle, whom we had not yet met, spent most of his time outdoors and we never did learn what his occupation or profession was, apart from his anti-German activities, which were numerous. They had a son who was away studying to be a doctor and came home occasionally at weekends.

'There are some Germans stationed in the town,' said Yves, 'but not many, and they don't interfere with the residents unduly, so you will be quite safe here, at the moment and very soon, I hope, on your way to Spain.'

Monsieur Denivelle still had not appeared and presently Yves and Charles pushed back their chairs and announced that they couldn't wait any longer as they had to get back to Paris that evening and must catch the next train. Just at that moment Gaston appeared in the garden and greeted our departing escorts who repeated their need to return to Paris and explaining that Eddy and I were the two 'parcels' of which he had been informed.

Gaston accompanied our friends through the garden, talking rapidly in French, and frequently casting backward glances towards us. I got the impression that he was not entirely satisfied with the situation and would have liked more information.

Returning into the dining room he spoke earnestly with Renée, his wife, who no doubt informed him of her conversation with Yves and Charles and the information they gave her concerning us. Turning to us, he shook hands and said we were welcome in his home, and on the morrow a number of friends were visiting and he wanted us to meet them. Renée sorted out some books, both French and English, showed us where we could find some indoor games, cards, chess and the like and we spent the evening quietly until dinner. After the meal Renée took us to our bedroom which, like the dining room, contained large, heavy furniture and an enormous double bed. She bade us goodnight and told us to remain in the bedroom in the morning until called.

When we were left alone, Eddy remarked, 'I don't think Gaston is very happy about us, he seems very doubtful. He's suspicious, and I bet these friends of his who he wants us to meet are a vetting committee.'

I agreed that our reception by Gaston hadn't been very enthusiastic and his attitude spelled of doubt.

'I suppose they've got to be careful, Eddy,' I said, 'After all we haven't a great deal of evidence to prove who we are. They've only got our word for it, and the word of the people in Paris. We've been lucky up to now and accepted by a lot of people. This chap is the only exception. Let's wait until tomorrow and see what happens.'

That first night in Ruffec, I remember very clearly. I didn't fall asleep for a long time as lots of unconnected thoughts whizzed through my mind. What kind of a night had it been in the pub at Nun Monkton, or Betty's Bar in York? Had any more chaps from the squadron gone missing since our do? The Christmas draw in the sergeants' mess would be taking place, and I had some tickets. If they were winners would they keep my prizes for me? What were my people at home doing or thinking at this moment? Where were the gunner, bomb-aimer and engineer? Had they survived? Did we really stand a chance of getting back to England? I didn't often say prayers, but I did that night, and more frequently afterwards, as well.

We were awakened the following morning by Madame Denivelle bringing us two bowls of coffee with biscuits.

'*Bon matin, mes amis*,' she greeted. '*Vous avez bien dormi?*' We replied that we had slept well and comfortably.

'You must remain in the bedroom,' she continued. 'Gaston will come to see you later when he wants you to come downstairs. Now I must go and attend my patients.'

Gaston came up about an hour later and indicated that we should follow him downstairs. Two men were seated at the dining table whom Gaston introduced as Lieutenant Peyraud of the local gendarmerie, the other being referred to simply as 'the Colonel'.

'*Mes amis*,' began Gaston, 'you understand it is essential to be very careful, so we would like you to answer one or two questions.' We were not asked to sit down, I noticed, and we stood together at the end of the table, waiting.

'What are your names, rank and numbers?' We told him. 'Where were you shot down?'

'Near Bar-le-Duc in the Meuse.'

'What aircraft were you flying?'

'A Halifax.'

'How many were there in your crew?' asked the Colonel.

'Seven.'

'What happened to the other five?' shot Gaston. We told him.

At this moment another younger man came into the dining room and exchanged the usual greeting.

'Ah, Monsieur Boulet,' said Gaston, 'these are the two English fliers brought from Paris yesterday. I would like you to speak to them in English please!'

André, for that was his name, proceeded to speak to us in very good English. He asked us in which part of England we lived, the name of the county, what nature of work we did before the war, did we have any hobbies and were we married? Then suddenly the tone of his voice changed and he barked out at us something which neither of us could understand, and after a pause I asked:

'Pardon, what did you say?'

He laughed and turning to Gaston and his friends said,

'*Ça va bien. Ils sont anglais, vraiment.*'

The tenseness in the atmosphere evaporated, and Gaston got up, came across to us, warmly shook hands and thumped our shoulders, and called Renée to fetch wine and glasses. Over the drinks we were put into the picture. Gaston was the leader of a Maquis group operating in the Charente department, and his two friends were also part of the group. André was the son-in-law of another member, not present at the moment, a Monsieur Grimaux, Gaston explained. He was sorry for his attitude when we arrived, but it was a necessary precaution as it was known that the Germans were cleverly infiltrating agents into Maquis groups and escape lines. He was now sure of us because André had suddenly said something to us in German, during the conversation and, had we been Germans, we would have reacted involuntarily, in an entirely different manner.

During the ensuing conversation that morning, we learned that Gaston and his friends were part of an organisation in direct contact with the SOE in London, through the efforts of an English lady called Mary Lindell, who frequently visited Ruffec. She was married to a Frenchman, the Comte de Milleville, and ran a small evasion line under her code-name Marie-Claire. This lady did actually visit Gaston during our stay, and probably had something to do with our subsequent movements, although I can't be sure about this. She was a very clever and courageous woman, who in spite of her arrest and imprisonment in Ravensbrück Concentration Camp managed to survive the war.

The next four days to Christmas were spent quietly in the house, reading, playing cards, chess and dominoes and we were allowed exercise in the courtyard. Gone were our hopes of celebrating Christmas in England, and instead a rather disturbing event was to take place in the Denivelle household on Christmas Eve.

It was customary, it seemed, to dine late on Christmas Eve, the meal extending into the early hours of 25 December and so celebrating the advent of Christmas Day. On this particular occasion the company consisted of M. and Mme Denivelle, their son Max, a chemist friend of the family and his wife, Mme Denivelle's housemaid and of course Eddy and I. About eleven o'clock we partook of the usual apéritifs and took our places round the table loaded with all sorts of goodies including goose, pigeon and hare plus all the trimmings. As a Christmas meal, it looked wonderful considering war-time rationing, but on the other hand most of it was home-reared and grown.

Monsieur Denivelle was not present as he was at the moment taking his dogs for their usual nightly exercise, but very soon he was in the courtyard and heard to come in through the kitchen and entered the dining room with his two spaniels. As he was about to take his place at the table, there was a thunderous banging at the kitchen door, and the unmistakable sound of German voices. Gaston leapt to his feet and disappeared into the kitchen where the intruders had by now entered. We all sat somewhat stunned by the sudden change in events and heard Gaston exchanging heated words with the Germans. In all towns and villages in France, a curfew was enforced by occupying troops, and Gaston had been seen by a German patrol entering the house well after the 10 pm curfew.

Not content with arguing in the kitchen, the patrol insisted on coming through into the dining room, still remonstrating with Gaston, who was expressing the fact that, being Christmas Eve, he had overlooked the lateness of the hour. The patrol consisted of three privates and an NCO and the latter glanced round the assembled company, then his eyes focussed on the table, loaded with Christmas fare, and for a moment there was silence. Then he spoke rapidly in German to the other three soldiers, and less rapidly in stumbling French to Gaston. The three privates then proceeded to remove most of the eatables from the table and wrapping them in serviettes disappeared through the kitchen and outside. The NCO with a further remonstrative remark to Gaston, and not another glance in our direction, turned and followed suit.

Had the situation not been so serious, so far as we were concerned, it could have been likened to a pantomime. As it was, the disappearance of the Christmas goodies meant less to us than the fact that fortunately we had not been spoken to by the Germans and probably recognised as Englishmen with the inevitable consequences of spending the rest of the war as prisoners, and the worse fate which would have befallen our gallant friends. The relief I experienced seeing the backs of those four soldiers sent an icy chill through my tensed sweating body.

So far as Gaston and his friends were concerned, their expressions were of anger and frustration rather than fear. Gaston went almost berserk, vowing vengeance on the morrow. Somewhat like Monsieur Roullier, of the restaurant in Paris, Gaston was well thought of by the local German commander of the area, to such an extent that he was not so popular with many local inhabitants, who viewed his apparent co-operation with the Germans very distastefully, little knowing of the active resistance in which he was participating. The following day he did actually complain to the officer in charge in Ruffec, and was promised that the necessary action would be taken against the German NCO responsible for the invasion of his privacy.

It was not long before another meal was prepared that evening, not so festive as the original, but very enjoyable, nevertheless, with Gaston mellowing as the evening progressed and gradually merged into Christmas morning.

Christmas Day was no different from any other day and we couldn't help but reminisce on what might be happening back in England on this festive occasion. Gaston was absent for most of the day and André Boulet called and had a chat with us. Gaston, he said, was an immensely courageous man, with an intense hatred of the Germans. His true patriotism and cool brain was an invaluable asset in the escape route and although he was not averse to working with Marie-Claire as her lieutenant and acting on orders, he had his own views on the way the line should be run and often put them into practice. Already he had personally escorted parties of airmen through various 'safe' houses to Toulouse and Varilhes, and contacted Spanish guides to get them over the Pyrenees. In between these hazardous excursions he fitted in acts of sabotage, the arranging of 'reception committees' for arms drops and the landing of agents.

'My part in all these activities is very small,' said André. 'But I am proud to be of some assistance.'

I have visited Ruffec a number of times since the war and still stay with Madame Denivelle in that same house in the square, and meet one or two other survivors of the group including Max Denivelle, her son, who is now a doctor in the town of Cognac, and Monsieur Boulet, now retired and living in Paris. Gaston died only a few years ago, and I too, admit to being happy and proud to have been associated with, and helped by such a gallant community.

Before André left that afternoon, I asked him to which 'line' he referred.

'The Pat line,' he said. 'The Pat O'Leary line, originally commenced in Marseilles as the starting point for an escape line via Perpignan and the Pyrenees. I believe O'Leary now operates from Toulouse also.'

All this information acted like a tonic upon us, and boosted our morale no end. Obviously danger still existed, but we felt ourselves to be in very good, capable hands.

CHAPTER EIGHT

Monique

It was around this time that we began to be moved about a bit, but always occasionally coming back to the Denivelles. I think always in the back of his mind, Gaston was perturbed about the Christmas Eve incident when we might easily have been discovered.

One place where we spent a day or two was with a local business man whose son was in the Resistance, and being a student of chemistry had proved himself useful in the field of explosives and homemade bombs in the period before British aircraft were dropping arms and explosives into the area. We never knew the name of this family – only the Christian names.

Another time we were accommodated in an empty house, having food brought to us by a friend of Gaston's whom we called 'Papa'.

Then it was decided to move us again, and one night we were taken stealthily by small paths and narrow lanes to a larger road. Our escort gave a low whistle and a figure appeared from the shadow of a high wall. He was introduced to us as Léon, a small, chunky man and obviously very strong. He guided us along by the high wall and we turned in to a narrow arched gateway leading into extensive private grounds. This proved to be a local château, still occupied by a marquis. In the grounds was a small cottage occupied by Léon, his wife and two daughters. Looked after very well by this family, we once more returned to the Denivelles' residence.

Being in the country and fairly isolated in some of these hideouts, we were able to pass the time sawing, cutting and splitting wood and storing it in dry sheds. Wood was the main source, for heat and cooking. We must have cut and stored tons of it and it proved good exercise. A lot of the time, particularly at M. Denivelle's we found it very boring, simply reading, playing endless games of patience and exercising out in the back garden, which was a long, narrow high-walled area, not overlooked by neighbouring property. It was undeniably tedious but we were superbly looked after and most comfortable. We were sure things were being done on our behalf; after all, they did not want us hanging around forever; it was in their interests to get us on our way, we were too much of a danger to them.

One day Gaston asked us how we felt about taking part in some minor action against the Germans, to relieve our boredom. It was entirely up to us, he said, and it was not without danger. We both jumped at the chance of taking some part in the group's activities and waited impatiently for an operation to take place in which we would join.

Cheering news was gleamed from the French newspapers which we could read each day, very laboriously, of course. The news was naturally all Vichy and German propaganda, but we could sometimes read between the lines and guess what was going on. Real news was given us by M. Denivelle from time to time after listening to the BBC (a strictly forbidden practice of course). Thus we were able to learn how the English Army, advancing 1200 miles since Alamein, had driven Rommel from his defensive position at Agheila and were continuing to pursue him further towards Tripoli, whilst the First Army were almost at the gates of Tunis, held up, unfortunately, by bad weather.

The good living, comfort and wholesome food we enjoyed in the various places where we were hidden in Ruffec, particularly the home of the Denivelles, proved a vital factor to the success of our subsequent journeyings in France, the Pyrenees and Spain. It would be impossible to explain properly the depth of gratitude and height of my esteem for these wonderfully brave French families.

Gaston spent very little time in the house. He was always away possibly dealing with his many business commitments, of which we learned very little, and probably also visited friends in surrounding villages who were also concerned with Resistance activities. Madame Denivelle, as a dentist had her patients to attend to during the day, so we were of necessity on our own most of the time, except for *la bonne*, Madame Denivelle's daily home-help, cook and general factotum, who obviously was trusted implicitly by Monsieur and Madame.

One evening, upon Gaston's return, as we were sitting down to the evening meal, he told us that he had sent a message to 'Marie-Claire.'

'She is the person who will arrange the next part of your journey. It is not her real name, but she is English.'

Two days later, he had to inform us that Marie-Claire had had an accident and was in hospital; her son was being contacted, but he was in Lyon.

We could do nothing but wait patiently and endure the usual boring routine. Occasionally we could not refrain from snapping at one another because we were an ill-assorted pair for conversation. Eddy was more of a townsman, whilst I dreamt of the freedom of the Northumberland countryside, and the mountains and Lakeland, of which he knew little. Practically the only common ground we had for discussion was history, a subject which we both liked.

Marie-Claire visited M. Denivelle one afternoon and I remember her as a handsome woman in her forties of medium height, greying hair and blue eyes. She looked very much out of place in the Denivelle dining room, talking with Gaston and his Resistance friends, because, although married to a Frenchman, and living in France for so long, she still looked and retained the typical characteristic of an English country lady, rather arrogant and a little masculine in manner. She still limped a little, as a result of her recent accident, and before leaving, she assured us that it would not be much longer before we would be on our way, via a new route, which had been opened up across the Pyrenees.

Diverting a little from our own experience in Ruffec, a rather more important event had been taking place, prior to our arrival, and even now, was not yet complete. This was the aftermath of the successful Commando Mission to blow up shipping at Bordeaux, using canoes and limpet mines. The Commandos were subsequently referred to as the Cockleshell Heroes. After the attack, the Commandos were to make their way to Ruffec, where they were told there would be an organisation equipped to get them out of France. Sadly there were only two survivors, Major Hasler and Corporal Sparks, and they made the successful journey to Ruffec, arriving there on 18 December, only two days before we ourselves arrived at M. Denivelle's.

On their arrival the two Commandos went to the Hôtel des Toques Blanches for a meal. There, they revealed their identities to the proprietor, who was not too sure of them at first, but after they had told their story were soon put in touch with another of Marie Claire's lieutenants, who hid them at a farm near the demarcation line, south of Ruffec, where they remained until the beginning of January. So while the Germans were on the lookout for these survivors they little knew that two English aircrew were also being hidden in the area. Gaston didn't play any part in this incident, as far as I know, but I'm sure he must have been aware of it. The two Commandos were successfully spirited out of France, and got back to England later in the year.

Later in the month we were finally given an opportunity to be included in a 'reception committee'.

'Tonight,' said Gaston, 'we expect an aircraft, bringing a French agent from England, to land a few miles north of the town and return with two Englishmen who have been operating in the Angoulême area. He explained in detail the arrangements for guiding in the aircraft by a simple system of hand-held torch lights, and the need for speed in getting the aircraft off again.

'We have used the field on frequent occasions, without alerting any interference, so there is no reason to suppose any trouble tonight.'

We left the house on bicycles before curfew time so as to be out into the open country where there were least likely to be patrols. Not far outside the town we were joined by three other Frenchmen, all members of Gaston's group, and after riding for another half hour arrived at a small farm close to the edge of a wood. Here, the bikes were parked behind a barn and we followed Gaston and his friends through the farmyard and into a fairly large field. It was quite light, the field being bathed in moonlight, and it was also extremely cold.

We had about an hour to wait before the aircraft was expected, during which period we were joined by the two agents who were going back to England. We flapped our arms, stamped our feet, tried running on the spot to keep warm, all the time thinking how marvellous it would be if that aircraft was coming to take us back. Not a chance, they wouldn't know yet that we were even alive, let alone here, on their reception field in France. I suggested to Gaston that he gave our names and numbers to the two blokes going back, and he said he would see what he could do. I didn't think anything came of it, because our people at home didn't receive any news until much later the following month.

Nearer the time, Gaston spaced out three lamp positions near the edge of the field furthest away from the farm building. The two main lamps were 150 yards apart allowing a clear approach, the third lamp position being placed at right angles to the second and approximately fifty yards away from it. When the aircraft was heard approaching, we and another torch-holder would position ourselves at these three points thus providing a make-shift flare-path and Gaston would flash the code letter inform-ing the pilot that all was in order to land.

The distant drone of a single-engined aircraft brought everyone alert, and we went to our respective positions. The aircraft, a Lysander, came over fairly low and Gaston flashed the signal and we steadily pointed the lit torches skywards. The aircraft circled once, the engine tone changing as the pilot throttled back, levelled out and came in to land. The landing was faultless and reaching the furthest light the pilot taxied in a quick tight circle to regain the point for take-off and I could see his passenger standing up in the cock-pit talking to the pilot, as he prepared to get out.

Suddenly the starboard wing of the Lysander dropped, nearly touching the grass, and the aircraft abruptly stopped, as the nose slewed round to the right. By this time, we were all close to the Lysander, and saw that the starboard wheel had sunk steeply into a large soft marshy patch of the field. The engine was revved madly but only served to make the wheel go deeper into the morass. As many of us who could got under the starboard wing by the under-carriage leg, lifted and pushed whilst the pilot gunned the engine to full power. But it was to no avail. The pilot closed the throttle and switched off. A deadly silence spread itself where before so much noise had existed, and I heard some choice English language issuing from the cock-pit.

The whole business should have been over in a few minutes, but now the audience was treated to quite an unusual ques-tionnaire.

The pilot levered himself up from his seat and began to address the reception committee in no uncertain manner.

'Who in all hell chose this bloody field?' he asked in carefully pronounced French, and with a strong English accent flavouring each word.

'Who is the boss of this crowd of yokels?'

His voice and accent, plus his grim determination to use his French to the best advantage, was music to my ears.

'The farm!' someone suddenly shouted. 'There might be some ropes or chains.'

Three people rushed across the field towards the farm, and in no time at all were on their way back accompanied by occupants of the farm with ropes and chains plus two heavy-looking horses. The ropes and chains were harnessed to the horses and the legs of the Lysander's under-carriage, and while the horses started pulling, everyone began pushing, puffing, panting and shouting advice to each other and to the horses. At the same time the pilot restarted his engine until the air reverberated with noise from excited French voices, the aircraft engine and the neighing of two horses who were desperately trying to break away from the din of the roaring engine behind them. Faintly through the hullabaloo the voice of the pilot could be heard again.

'For Christ's sake!' he bellowed. 'Put a sock in it. You'll have the whole bloody German army here at any minute.'

If anyone heard him, they ignored what he said and continued to push, pant and shout excitedly. I continually kept glancing towards the road and approaches to the farm expecting to see the headlights and hear the exhausts of official Citroëns, belonging to the security police, or the arrival of a German army unit to investigate the uproar. This was supposed to be a clandestine operation, I thought, carried out secretly and with minimum of noise but it had developed into something resembling a comic opera. Had the situation not been so serious and dangerous, it would have been hilarious. The pilot was still swearing and voicing typical RAF epithets to all and sundry when, suddenly the wheel became unstuck, the horses nearly going on their knees as the load lessened, and the wheel slithered out of the morass onto firm ground. The two homeward-bound agents began throwing their meagre belongings into the cock-pit and bidding their French colleagues goodbye.

'Now what the hell's going on down there?' yelled the pilot, his patience rapidly becoming exhausted. 'Get into the bloody aircraft and let's get the hell out of here.'

The two men quickly clambered up into the aircraft, we took up the flare path positions and the aircraft turned, its engine opened up, the pilot raised his hand in a gesture of farewell, and the little Lysander roared off across the field, swiftly to be swallowed up in the night sky. The incoming French agent was nowhere to be seen, having sensibly put as much distance as possible between himself and the recent jamboree, before the Wehrmacht arrived and broke up the party.

In spite of the recent uproar, the enemy did not appear, and we retrieved our bikes and rode back to Ruffec without further incident. The event could have had serious repercussions we knew, but we couldn't help but see the funny side. Gaston was not amused.

We participated in one or two more events of a similar nature, but these went off quite smoothly. Over night we helped in the retrievement of packages of small arms and ammunition dropped by parachute. On another evening we were allowed to sit in on a meeting held in the Hôtel de France in Ruffec, when a number of Resistance leaders from outlying areas of the Charente were discussing some kind of sabotage or ambush operation designed to take place at a future date. We were not acquainted with full details of the actual operation, but it helped to relieve our boredom, and gave us an insight into the way that the underground warfare was being waged.

One day, later in the month, one of Gaston's friends arrived with a camera, and our photographs were taken, passport size, and these, they told us, would be used for spurious identity papers. Two or three days later Yves unexpectedly arrived from Paris and Gaston informed us that it was essential that we return to Paris without delay, where we would be issued with our identity cards before proceeding further on our journey. We were completely nonplussed on this issue. Another hazardous train journey back to Paris seemed to us a retrograde step, and we wondered why the identity cards couldn't have been brought to Ruffec by Yves. But it was not for us to question or criticize the methods of our helpers, the drill was to do as we were told without question.

Apparently it was too late that day to catch a suitable train from Ruffec to Paris, although we could sense that both Yves and Gaston would have been happier if we had been able to depart almost immediately. I wondered what had happened to the original plan concerning Marie-Claire and her son and the newly opened route across the Pyrenees. Of course, she may have been in collusion with Yves and his group in Paris and, for reasons unknown to us it was necessary to return to Paris. It certainly seemed a peculiar way to operate an escape line.

Yves arranged to stay at the Hôtel de France in Ruffec as Madame Denivelle had not a spare room or bed. However, in the evening a farewell dinner was put on for us which Yves attended before going to the Hôtel. It was a most enjoyable evening but with an undertone of sadness on our part, to be leaving these good people, and we crawled into bed at a very late hour, and not a little drunk.

In the morning, after the usual French breakfast, Yves arrived, and we said our good-byes to the Denivelles, trying our best to express our gratitude for their kindness. Madame Denivelle presented each of us with a small Lourdes medallion and a tiny bottle of perfume called *Je suis là* for our wives. The medallions, she said, would ensure our safe journey across the Pyrenees. Yves then escorted us to the station where we boarded the train bound for Paris. Our previous two journeys by train from Vitry-le-François to Paris, and Paris to Ruffec had fortunately been uneventful considering we had no official papers. We still did not have identity papers, only prints of the passport photos taken at Ruffec for spurious *Cartes Identités* when these became available. Little did we think that this journey was to prove somewhat different.

The first stop was at Poitiers and a minute or two after leaving that station, Yves appeared at the door of our compartment, making urgent gestures for us to leave our seats and come into the corridor. Normally of a very wan complexion, he now looked like death.

'A German Police Control has boarded the train at Poitiers,' he said. 'They are starting at the front of the train and checking all passengers for papers. There is nothing I can do about it.' He paused and drew a deep breath, then continued; 'You have two alternatives, as I see it. Sit tight and allow yourselves to be arrested. You still have your service identity tags and will merely be made prisoners of war or' – he paused again, 'you can choose to leave the train before they reach this carriage, and risk the consequences.'

Eddy looked at me, then back to Yves. 'You mean make a jump for it?' he said.

'Yes,' replied Yves 'there's nothing else for it. Now I must leave you, I cannot risk being seen talking to you. I'm sorry, very sorry. *Au revoir et bon chance.*'

He made his way back along the corridor while we stood, looking at one another, stunned at the reversal of good fortune.

'Well. What is it to be?' I demanded.

'I don't know about you, Robbie,' Eddy breathed, 'but I'm not letting this lot take me prisoner now: after getting so far. This bloody train isn't travelling so fast at the moment. We might get away with it. Let's move down towards the rear.'

We moved quickly away along the corridor and into the next coach. Here we were met by a crowd of youths pushing along the corridor in the opposite direction, and we became separated. I remembered that we had boarded the train in either the second or third coach from the engine, and since the control were checking the train from the front end, they would soon be entering the coach in which I now was. Eddy was somewhere ahead. I had now reached the door at the end of the coach and gazed out at the countryside passing by the window. True, the train was not travelling really fast and there appeared to be a rising gradient. The line for trains travelling in the opposite direction was on this side so I crossed the carriage to the other side. Eddy was right. Having got so far, all the help we had been given would be in vain. If we were captured then there was the possibility of interrogation as to how we had got so far, who had helped and given us the clothing we now wore. The answer would have to be name, rank and number, nothing more. But would our captors be satisfied with such an answer? That again would depend upon who our captors would be. German military authorities or the Gestapo. If the latter, I knew they would be pretty nasty. Better to jump, I decided.

Then suddenly, as I put my hand on the door handle, I remembered the doors at each end of the coach on the French railways were well inset into the side of the coach body, unlike the doors on British trains, which were flush with the sides of the coach. Furthermore, there were two long vertical brass handholds, one each side of the doorway, and there were three steps down almost to rail level because French station platforms were so low. With luck I could perhaps hang on to the holds, whilst standing on the bottom step and my head would be below the window and out of sight unless anyone looked out of the train and this was unlikely since windows on French trains did not drop down as they did on British coaches. This all went through my head in a flash.

I pulled open the door, stepped backwards through it, found a foothold on the first step, grabbed a hand-hold with one hand, and pulled the door shut with the other. I then lowered myself on to the next step and then the last one. My head was well below window level. I might have thought the train was not travelling at any great speed, but, hanging on, outside the door, I felt we must be doing at least a ton. I hung on like grim death, the wind tearing at my clothing whilst passing anything like a signal gantry or lineside hut, caused a suction which threatened to pull me off. I doubt whether I would have held on if I had been on the other side and passed another train going south. The suction would have been too strong. I eventually managed to push my legs between the bottom two steps and was able to sit on the bottom one, taking the strain off my legs and partially off my arms.

It was now a case of wondering how long I should remain in this position and when to re-enter the coach hoping the Control had passed. Where was Eddy? Had he jumped or changed his mind and given up? Also I could not afford to be hanging on like this when we arrived at the next station.

I stuck it for about twenty minutes I think, then eased myself carefully up to window level. It was clear inside, but I could not see along the corridor and I could hear nothing because of the roar of the wind outside. Better wait a little longer I decided, and dropped down again. I gave it another ten minutes. They would surely be finished in the front three coaches by now; there had not been many passengers on the train at Ruffec, although I had no idea how many had joined at Poitiers.

I heaved myself up, pushed open the door and crawled over the step onto the floor of the coach. There was not a soul in the corridor as I pulled the door shut and literally fell into the lavatory compartment and bolted the door. I sat on the lavatory pan, quite exhausted, breathing deeply and gradually pulled myself together. After a few minutes I became aware of the train slowing down, and let myself out of the toilet compartment. The train slowly came to a halt at St Pierre-des-Corps.

Opening the door I looked forward along the train expecting to see Eddy being escorted off the train by the Police Control. I observed a man in German military uniform alight, accompanied by a civilian in a dark suit and Trilby hat and they were joined by what appeared to be a railway ticket collector. I also saw Yves. He also was looking forward along the train. Then the train began moving off and I fairly ran along the corridor through the coaches to where I thought Yves was and finally located him. To say he was astonished would be putting it mildly.

'*Mon Dieu*,' he muttered, '*comment, mais comment ...?*' he spluttered.

I quickly explained and then asked if the three men I had seen alighting were the Police Control party. He said they were. Then I said, 'then where the hell is Eddy?'

We sat down in an empty compartment and I again told him what I had done. If Eddy had jumped then I had not seen him, but anyway I had been too occupied hanging on to notice anyone fall, jump or be lying on the railside.

Shortly, a uniformed figure passed the compartment, stopped, turned back and opened the sliding door. It was the train conductor. He looked quizzically at me, switched his gaze to Yves and said, '*Venez, si vous plait, venez avec moi.*'

Yves left his seat and followed the conductor back along the train to the rear. A few minutes later he returned and with him was Eddy, a wide grin on his face. That was the first time that I had ever seen Eddy really laugh or look pleased about anything. The train conductor was also with them, and we sat down in the empty compartment while Eddy recounted what had happened.

Apparently after being separated from me, he had continued walking the full length of the train contemplating and trying to make up his mind which action to take. He had eventually reached the last vehicle and opening the connecting vestibule door found himself in the baggage car, where sat the train conductor. It was here that another idea suddenly occurred to Eddy, and he had blurted out to the conductor, '*Je suis anglais, un aviateur. Pouvez vous m'assister?*'

The surprised conductor was not aware that a Police Control had boarded the front of the train at Poitiers until Eddy explained this to him. The conductor taken by surprise and off-guard, spoke '*Anglais?*' he said, dubiously. '*Oui, oui,*' replied Eddy and pulled his identity tags from his collar and showed them to the railwayman, who appeared satisfied.

There was very little passengers' luggage in the car but at one end was stacked a large quantity of crates and cardboard cartons. Some of the crates contained live chickens – others eggs and fruit and were quite bulky.

'*Au derrière,*' said the conductor. 'Behind the crates and remain there until I give the word.'

Eddy could hardly believe his good fortune and dived behind the piled crates and boxes. Like me, after a while he was conscious of the train reducing speed and eventually coming to a stop. There was no movement in the car, no indication of anyone entering and speaking to the conductor and Eddy remained, squatting behind the crates. Soon the train got underway again and the railwayman called.

'*Ça va bien, mon ami, venez.*' It is all right now.

Eddy emerged from his hide-out and began to tell the conductor about me and what we had originally intended to do. There upon the conductor set off along the train until he located the compartment as I have already described. Apparently the Police Control party had not even entered the baggage car. They rarely did, the conductor said, unless they had good reason and were searching for something specific. We learned that he was a widower, and lived with his daughter in a flat near the Gare du Nord, but never mentioned his name. He was pleased that he had been of some assistance to us, wished us luck and took his leave to return to his duties.

By this time I had recovered my composure, but Eddy continued to see the funny side of the predicament I had been subjected to. Naturally I did not see anything amusing about the incident and could only be thankful we had both got away with it, irrespective of the methods adopted.

We arrived back in Paris early in the afternoon, after that

eventful journey, and were met by Charles who received us quite cheerfully, not in the least perturbed by our second visit to the French capital, and the problems which could be incurred.

'You enjoyed your stay in Ruffec with M. and Mme Denivelle?' he asked. 'They are good friends of my family. Lieutenant Peyraud of the Ruffec Gendarmerie is also a good friend,' he added, 'and it is on his advice that you have now returned to Paris. Both he and M. Denivelle are convinced that a traitor exists in the Ruffec area, or, at least, someone is talking too much. A farm near to Bordeaux was suddenly raided by a Security Police Unit, and a French undercover radio operator who was operating from there was arrested and is now in the hands of the Gestapo. A family living in Limoges was visited by the Gestapo and accused of hiding allied servicemen. Fortunately they were later released due to lack of evidence. If the captured radio operator is made to talk, a lot of people could be in great danger. It was therefore decided that you should be got out of the area without delay, and, at the moment, Paris is as safe as anywhere.'

So there we had it, the reason for our return journey to Paris, without asking for it. I didn't feel in the least elated and thought I would rather not have known about the intrigue, conspiracy and possible treacherous behaviour with which we were surrounded. Reading fiction stories about such goings-on was great, but this was for real, and therefore mentally disturbing, to say the least.

Yves then proceeded to explain that arrangements had been made for our second stay in the capital and we would cross the city by the Metro, getting off at Les Sablons station. At Les Sablons, we were to be handed over to another member of the group, who would take us to a 'safe house'. The journey across Paris was a long one, and an uncomfortable one, it now being the beginning of the city rush hour.

'There's safety in numbers,' whispered Eddy sagely. 'We won't look, or feel half so conspicuous in among this lot.'

We had to change lines at Bastille, and it was with considerable difficulty that we were able to keep contact with our two escorts. At Les Sablons Metro we entered a small café just outside the station entrance. Yves motioned us to a corner table where we sat quietly until a small stout man appeared from double glass doors behind the counter. He beckoned us to follow into a small, sparsely furnished room where he brought coffees for the four of us. He seemed a bit edgy and not too pleased, as if he hadn't been expecting us at that moment.

'Wait here,' he said, 'I must be sure of your identity. This gentleman will see that you remain.' He opened a communicating door into a room which revealed a uniformed Gendarme. There was an uncomfortable period of silence. Were we in the right hands? Had we been brought to the wrong cafe? Which side was this Gendarme on? But our anxieties were quickly dispelled when Charles cried:

'It is not necessary, *Monsieur*. This gentleman knows who I am, all is well,' and addressing the Gendarme: '*Bonjour, Emile, comment allez vous*? We are meeting Georges here, but I think we have arrived too early.'

The Gendarme smiled, and with a few words to the café proprietor, put that anxious gentleman's mind at rest, whereupon he happily disappeared back into the main café.

'Georges is likely to be a little late,' said Emile, 'some delay at the office, and he asked me to come to the café to meet you and make sure all was in order. You have come from Ruffec today, I believe. How are things down there?'

'Another one of the gang,' I remarked to Eddy. 'I got a bit worried when I saw him at first.'

'Yes. I wondered whether somebody had dropped a clanger, but he seems to know all about the set up. Wonder who Georges is?'

Yves, Charles and Emile continued their conversation over more coffee, until the arrival of Georges within quarter of an hour. He was slightly built, dark and clean-shaven. He wore a light grey suit and suede shoes, a silk shirt and a dark blue bow tie. He looked like a very successful business executive; and probably was. We never did find out his true calling. Like most of the French people we had encountered up to now, he asked us a lot of questions in English about our journey, our home life and families, seeming to be well satisfied with our answers.

'Now we must leave,' he said eventually, and bidding farewell to Yves and his companions he left the room and went into the main café. At the door he turned to us and said:

'You must follow me at a safe distance. If I stop you must divert, then follow me when I set off again. Have nothing to do with me, just follow and when I enter into the doorway of a flat in Rue Perronet – note the number, walk past to the end of the street, then return and enter.'

He moved off and we followed at a discreet distance and before long reached the Rue Perronet, and saw him enter number 46. We did as instructed, returned up the street and turned into the entrance. Here, he was waiting in the hallway, behind a closed glass door, and led us to a selected door. Carefully he pressed the bell button three times rapidly, followed by a short pause and a further two slower rings.

In a moment it was opened by a lady in hospital nurse's uniform who smiled warmly at Georges and beckoned us in. We didn't know it then, but this was the threshold to a highly efficient evasion line across the Pyrenees. It was the 'Brandy Zone Nord Line' leading eventually into the famous 'Pat' line.

Monique Spiquel was the lady's name, although I was not to know this until long after the end of the war. She was slight and dark, and looked immaculate in a hospital uniform, with a red cross on the breast. She greeted Georges with warmth and he returned her greeting with equal affection before turning round to introduce Eddy and me. She welcomed us to her flat and hoped it would help us on our way. It was only a tiny two-roomed flat, reasonably furnished and with a small alcove which housed a cooker and wash basin.

'We have to be careful here about noise,' said Monique. 'It is important that people in the neighbouring flats do not become aware that there are strangers using the flat, so tread quietly preferably in stocking feet and keep away from the windows. Most of the time, you will be alone in the flat and any callers will know the code ring – three quick rings, or knocks followed by two slower. Other than this ignore any rings and keep very quiet. I have a friend who has a key to the flat and will visit you frequently to prepare a meal in my absence while you are here. I will be sleeping either at my friend's flat or at the hospital where I work, but I'll visit you as much as possible. No doubt you will find the inactivity very boring but that cannot be helped, and it will not be for long I hope. Now we will have some coffee.'

As we sat drinking coffee she continually asked questions about our experiences, since leaving Levoncourt and our first arrival in Paris, occasionally turning to Georges and conversing in rapid French. The names Ruffec, Bergerac, demarcation line and Toulouse featured largely in the conversation so we concluded it was our future that was under discussion.

Presently Monique said, 'Now I must leave for the hospital. Georges will stay with you for a while and I will see you tomorrow.'

We spent the remainder of the day in the flat, talking with Georges until Monique's friend arrived with a ready cooked meal for the three of us. After the meal Georges left saying that he too would see us on the morrow. Monique's friend, a much younger person, busied herself washing up and generally tidying the flat, bade us goodnight and left.

Left on our own, we couldn't help thinking and talking about the inconvenience we were causing Monique. She had virtually given up her comfortable flat in order to ensure our well being and safety and at the same time putting herself in grave danger. I thought of Nurse Cavell who during the 1914 war, faced a firing squad for similar activity.

George had told us that from now onwards we would be referred to as 'parcels', and as such had to be examined carefully before acceptance for 'posting' down the line. We could have been parcels which were lethal and ready to explode at any time, he said, hence the extreme care regarding our identities. From the information he and Monique had received from Ruffec, they were satisfied that we were above suspicion.

There was a good selection of paper backs available in the flat, mainly by such authors as Edgar Wallace and Sydney Horler and we spent the rest of that evening either reading or playing draughts, finally deciding sleep was next on the agenda. The bedroom contained a single bed only, so we tossed for it. I lost and spent the night on the settee where I slept soundly, feeling much easier in mind about our situation and progress.

We were awakened next morning by Monique's friend letting herself into the flat, and preparing two bowls of coffee and bread rolls. She busied herself around the flat and soon left, leaving all the ingredients of a cold meal for our lunch.

The remainder of that day was spent again reading, playing cards or chess. We both had a bath of sorts, standing up in the little alcove, using a minute piece of soap, and felt cleaner and fresher as a result.

Monique arrived in the early evening, having finished her turn of duty at the hospital, and immediately set to preparing an evening meal. It was difficult to believe that this slight attractive woman was the leader of an escape line which entailed the hiding of potentially dangerous visitors, like ourselves in her flat. She could speak very little English but nevertheless the evening was spent pleasurably eating, drinking and talking in general terms about the war, the conduct of the German soldiery in Paris and the mood of the civilian population back in England undergoing the onslaught of frequent German air raids.

At the conclusion of the meal, which as usual was quite late, we helped Monique to wash up, a task which few Frenchmen would ever engage in, she said, and soon it was time for her to leave to make her way to her friend's flat and spend the night there.

'Tomorrow,' she said, 'we will have a lunch party here in the flat, and you will meet some of my colleagues. Until then *bonsoir et dormez bien*', and she left, quickly reminding us of the door bell code and the need for quietness.

Late the following morning she returned to the flat and immediately began preparing the mid-day meal assisted by her friend. Later the code ring sounded at the door and the first visitor was admitted. He reminded me of Adolphe Menjou, the well known pre-war French actor. He greeted Monique with exaggerated courtesy and elegance, and turning his eyes on us, remarked:

'*Bonjour, bonjour, mes enfants, comment allez vous?*'

As we returned the greetings, Monique introduced him as Mario, and he was a lawyer by profession.

'These are your two new packages for our postbag to Spain?' he enquired of Monique.

'Yes,' she replied. 'They arrived two days ago from Ruffec. We had word from Peyraud, that certain things were going wrong in the Charente, particularly since the British Commando raid in Bordeaux harbour and it was better for these two Englishmen to be evacuated. We now have to replan.'

Mario nodded. 'And Gaston?' he asked.

'Gaston agreed without hesitation. By now he should have been in touch with Pat in Marseilles on the question of future operations.'

Mario lapsed into silence, clearly upset by this news from Ruffec.

We had not long to wait for the next visitors who were Georges accompanied by another more elderly man, heavily bearded but completely bald on top. This was Victor and he was a Roman Catholic priest. Monique produced bottles and glasses and we all took places at the dining table for apéritifs. The last guest to arrive was a tall, wiry young man with a distinct air of confidence and self-assertion but at the same time oozed humour and friendliness and was introduced as Jacques. He smoked continuously, even during the meal, between courses.

Between them Monique and Mario told the others of the trouble at Ruffec resulting in our return to Paris, explaining that Gaston was reporting to Pat at Marseilles for instructions.

'Pat is not now at Marseilles,' interrupted Jacques. 'He has taken up residence in Toulouse and has been in touch with London regarding money and arms and has no doubt referred to the Ruffec upsets also. Future 'parcels' must be sent to Toulouse.

The word 'London' startled me. These people, this line also was in touch with London? Does 'London' know we are with these people I wondered, and had our families at home been informed? I hoped so, but I didn't dare ask, there were more important things at stake than our two bodies, and anyway we were not out of the wood yet, not by a long chalk. Discussing the situation between ourselves when we were alone, we were convinced of the efficiency of the organisation in spite of the inner feeling of frustration at our own inactivity. Not unnaturally, we occasionally 'had words' due to getting on one another's nerves.

The meal at Monique's that day was superb, and over coffee and cognac, a lively discussion took place between our five friends, very little of which we were able to comprehend fully, but a lot of which concerned us. I'm certain, since the words, papers, identity and photo cropped up frequently.

Soon Mario and Victor took their leave, leaving us with Monique, Georges and Jacques.

'It is necessary that identity cards be prepared for you before the next part of your journey is attempted,' said Monique. 'For that, photographs are required, so we will go to a photographer friend this afternoon and obtain these.'

'But, Madame,' I interjected, 'we had identity photos taken by a photographer in Ruffec.'

'They are not suitable,' Monique answered, 'for the type of identity card issued by the German authorities in Paris, and have been destroyed.'

In a few minutes we left the flat with Monique, walked a short distance down the street to the shop of a woman photographer. The woman showed no surprise when Monique stated her requirements, but I swear that she was only too well aware or at least suspicious of our identities. She developed and handed over passport sized photos within minutes. We then carried on to the Préfecture where Monique knew a senior Inspector, and after talking her way past one or two subordinates reached the Inspector's private office where he reluctantly agreed to supply the necessary identity cards. We then returned to the flat, where Georges and Jacques were still waiting.

The arrangements were that we would leave for Toulouse as soon as possible after the identity cards were prepared. One difficulty had yet to be overcome however, that being crossing the demarcation line into what had previously been the unoccupied zone. The German forces had crossed the line in November 1942 and so occupied the whole of France. The imaginary line still existed however and continued to be patrolled although not so thoroughly, and Toulouse lay to the south of the line. On the outskirts of the town in Bergerac, there was known to be a 'safe house' whose grounds extended over the line and it was to this destination we were to proceed.

CHAPTER NINE

Crossing the Demarcation Line

The forged identity cards were delivered to us two days later, and the following day we again left Paris, this time, we hoped, to complete our journey to Spain. A young boy arrived at the flat in the early evening to conduct us to Austerlitz railway station. We had previously said our goodbyes to Monique earlier in the day, because she was on duty at the hospital, that evening and night.

Little did I know that, unlike a number of our helpers, I was to renew acquaintance with this brave lady, 41 years later, in an extraordinary manner. In 1983 she discovered among some papers, copies of the passport photos of Eddy and me. She wrote to the RAF Escaping Society giving details of the events in 1942 and the Society printed photocopies in the normal newsletter sent to members. Recognising myself, I wrote to the Society, who gave me her address, which turned out to be the same flat where I had been hidden, and I was able to visit her and also meet Georges and Jacques once more. Now in her eighties, she told me that later in 1942 the Gestapo had arrived at the flat and arrested her, bundled her into a car bound for their Paris Headquarters in Avenue Foch and subsequent interrogation. During the journey she had thrown herself out of the car whilst in traffic, mingled with passers-by and successfully escaped. Eventually getting to England with Georges, they worked with British Intelligence until D-Day when they returned to France and assisted the Allies during the Liberation. She received decorations from British, French and American sources, of which she is very proud.

Arriving at the station, we found Jacques impatiently waiting for us, having already been to the booking window and bought the necessary train tickets. He was to act as our courier on the journey and, it seems, this was his first assignment as such, so was, not unnaturally, rather nervous, this being indicated by the large number of cigarette butts scattered at his feet. A handshake for each of us was a means of passing us our train tickets and we passed through the barrier to the departure platform where the train was already waiting. It was a corridor train and by now all the coaches were full and many passengers were standing in the corridors, amongst them a number of uniformed Germans. We squeezed into one coach and Jacques into the adjacent one. It was going to be a four hour journey, at least, our destination being Libourne, just short of Bordeaux.

The first stop was Les Aubrais (for Orléans) where very few passengers alighted, but many more boarded the train. I tried to reassure myself that with the corridors being packed so tightly with humanity, it would be almost impossible for a police check to take place. However, the next stop was at St Pierre-des-Corps (for Tours) and here large numbers of passengers left the train, a lot of them Germans. It was still impossible to find a seat, and we sat on the floor in the corridor. After another stop at Poitiers the train was much less crowded but evidently a travelling ticket inspector had boarded the train and shouts could be heard as he pushed along the corridor, followed by two railway police. We watched the men work their way towards us and noted the inspector merely asked for tickets, but occasionally the police demanded identity papers. This could be it, I thought, the first test of our recently acquired identity cards, and I muttered a prayer.

Next to Eddy an elderly man was seated on a suitcase. As the officials approached he began showing signs of fear and apprehension.

'*Votre billet, si vous plait!*' said the collector.

The man fumbled in a worn purse and produced a ticket of sorts and a piece of paper. The collector thrust the ticket back angrily and passed the slip of paper to the police, one of whom shouted something at the man, then turned and harangued the ticket collector. The man was pulled unceremoniously to his feet and jostled back down the corridor towards the rear of the train. The second policeman picked up the suitcase and followed whilst the ticket collector demanded our tickets, glanced briefly at them and gave them back without a word. He moved on and into the next coach.

We heaved sighs of relief. Whether our spurious identity

cards would have satisfied the trained eyes of the police we were not to know, a fear-stricken elderly man had prevented their examination, and for what reason, we were not to know either.

After passing through Angoulême, we spotted Jacques at the end of the corridor walking towards us, and as he passed, whispered that the next stop would be ours.

It was now late afternoon and beginning to get dark when we alighted at Libourne, and following a pre-arranged programme, Jacques joined us outside the station and led us to the Hôtel de l'Orient, which evidently belonged to one of his friends.

During the course of the evening, the hotelier was visited unexpectedly by a friend who informed him that the German Security Police in the area, planned to visit the hotel that very evening to verify identities of all occupants, visitors and staff alike. Jacques immediately decided that having been forewarned, it would be safer not to remain in the hotel and we hurriedly left to seek out a farm a mile or two distant, at St Martin de Gurgon, the home of M. Pierrefiche, another acquaintance of Jacques. As we walked, it began to rain. A cold wind blew from the north bringing with it a fine steady rain which whipped our faces and very soon penetrated our clothing. Jacques' spirits were not to be dampened.

'Soon we will arrive at the farm,' he said. 'They are very good friends of mine and will see to it that we get dry clothing, probably a bath, and certainly a meal and a bed for the night.'

'I hope he's right,' muttered Eddy. 'I could eat a horse and I'm dying for a drink.'

I agreed, and although I was ready to eat almost anything, the prospect of a bath appealed to me more.

Presently we came to a lane leading off the road, which was the private approach to the farm. The end of the lane was closed by a wide five barred gate and beyond was the farm yard. Across the yard was the farmhouse with a smoking chimney and surrounded by several sheds and barns. Jacques strode to the door, knocked quietly and, after a few seconds, it was opened by an elderly man. He held the door half open and peered at us standing in the darkness of the farm yard.

'*Qu'est-ce que vous voulez?*' he began, and then when his eyes became adjusted to the darkness, '*Mon Dieu, c'est Jacques! Comment allez vous, Jacques? Que faites vous ici? Entrez, entrez!*'

He held the door open fully allowing us to follow Jacques into the kitchen where a woman was busy at a stove, from which an appetising smell was wafting.

'*Bonjour, Jacques!*' she exclaimed. 'You have friends with you?' she added in an enquiring tone of voice.

'*Oui, Madame,*' Jacques answered. 'Please don't be alarmed, they are English airmen, evading capture and trying to reach Spain over the mountains.'

The woman glanced at her husband who was now wearing a very worried expression in place of the cheerful surprise he had expressed when he first saw Jacques. He didn't say anything but gazed rather anxiously at the two of us, then turned to Jacques and addressed him in rapid French, gesturing wildly as he spoke.

The woman spoke again. 'You are sure, Jacques?' she asked. 'You are certain that they are not –' She broke off as Jacques interrupted her.

'*Non, Madame.* They are definitely Englishmen. Every precaution has already been taken. You have nothing to fear on that score.'

'*Ça va bien,*' she replied. 'Sit down please, I expect you are ready to eat and we are just about to have dinner.' She indicated three chairs and we pulled these to the table and sat down. Jacques commenced speaking again to the couple relating the full account of our time in Paris, the arrival at the Hôtel de l'Orient and the reason for the hasty departure and arrival here.

The state of tension in the atmosphere rapidly evaporated as Jacques talked, and the husband seemed resigned to accepting the situation and the action of his wife. Soon we had large plates of soup and slices of French bread before us. The soup was plentiful, followed by a luscious piece of boiled ham with vegetables and finally salad.

After the meal her husband excused himself and disappeared through a back entrance, leaving his wife alone with us in the kitchen. We were able to relate to her in the best French we could muster, our adventure of the past few weeks and the hopes that soon we would get to Toulouse and eventually over the Pyrenees and into Spain. She was clearly impressed by our story and also by the account given her by Jacques, who it seemed, was a native of this area in the Dordogne and was a friend of long standing. She hadn't known, however, until now that Jacques was an active member of the resistance and the escape line organisation, but she and her husband knew that there were certain active elements in Libourne and Bergerac who were working against the Nazis.

The fact that we were quite wet after our walk from Libourne had been overlooked due to the lengthy conversation and the meal. Jacques had fared better than us since he wore a mackintosh, and it was only when we both involuntarily shivered that Madame Pierrefiche realised how wet we were and apologised profusely for the oversight. She disappeared hastily, and returned with some dry clothing and two rough towels. We undressed unashamedly by the stove, and donned the dry garments.

'These will dry overnight,' she said, 'and be ready to wear again tomorrow. You will sleep here tonight, Jacques, in the house, and the Englishmen must sleep in one of the barns. They will be all right there, quite comfortable, and no one will disturb them.' She provided us with two heavy blankets, which, together with the straw in a small barn, proved to be ideal. It was still raining, more heavily now, pattering on the roof and echoing eerily round the barn. I prayed it would dry up in the morning when we would probably have some more walking to do to cross the demarcation line, wherever that might be.

We were awake, when Mme Pierrefiche came to the barn.

'*Bonjour, mes enfants*, she greeted. '*Vous avez bien dormi?*' We replied saying we had slept well, and asked if the weather was improved.

'*Mais oui,*' she said. 'The weather is good and you must come to the house where you can shave, wash and have breakfast, then we will tell you what must be done.'

Jacques and M. Pierrefiche were seated having breakfast in the kitchen when we entered the house, and conversing volubly in French at a rate which was far beyond our capability to understand. We changed into our clothing, now quite dry, washed thoroughly and shaved, returning quickly to the kitchen where we breakfasted on coffee, bread and marmalade.

'You will leave here in the back of a small van which will take you nearly into Bergerac,' said M. Pierrefiche. 'It will take about one and a half hours, I shall be driving. At a certain point I will tell you to get out; no one will see you alight at this spot. Jacques will remain with you, until a girl appears on a bicycle, passes the van and continues towards Bergerac. Jacques knows what the girl looks like and will indicate the fact to you, then he will leave you. You will follow the girl who will soon stop outside a certain house, make some adjustment to her cycle, then cycle away. You will then go to that house and knock or ring. It will be answered by an old lady who will admit you. That's all. You must then take instructions from her. Good luck, and safe journey to England.'

Madame Pierrefiche then bade us farewell and asked that we write to her after the war, showing that we had been successful. I did indeed write as requested, but received no reply and my letter was not returned.

Everything went according to plan, and we scrambled out of the little van when it turned into a narrow opening on the right. The houses on the outskirts of the town were visible a few hundred yards further on. Almost immediately a dark-haired teenage girl appeared riding a bicycle along the road which we had just come, passed the opening and carried on. Jacques nodded and gave a thumbs up sign. His job was now finished, he returned to the van, which drove off.

We set off, following the bicycle which was proceeding fairly slowly towards the town. She turned a corner to the left and as we neared the corner, perceived her stooping over the bike, fiddling with the chain or pedals. On seeing our approach, she remounted the bike and carried on, without a word or sign of recognition. Since climbing out of the van, we had seen no one, and I'm sure we had not been observed. The spot had been picked with care. The only person visible now was a postman making his deliveries.

Reaching the house opposite the place where the girl had stopped, we pushed open the gate and rang the door bell once.

During that brief period whilst awaiting for an answer to our ring, the unreality of our situation passed through my mind, much as it had during the past few weeks. I couldn't help remembering books I had read, involving espionage, treachery, mystery and hare-brained schemes brilliantly evolved by the thriller writers of the period. Here we were, a couple of British Servicemen, through no fault of our own, finding ourselves in a not dissimilar environment, listening and acting upon coded door knocks, being passed clandestinely from one hide-out to another, by nameless people whom we could only but trust and trying to remember details of our new identities, as per forged cards, in case we were challenged. No it wasn't a fiction thriller, it was real all right. I meditated on the future, what other areas we had yet to enter and difficulties to surmount. I suppose Eddy must have felt very much the same, at times, although he never gave voice to his thoughts, and if I speculated on the possible outcome, he was never very keen to prolong any discussion.

My reverie was brought to a conclusion when the door was opened by an elderly lady, tall and slim and wearing a welcoming smile.

'Come in,' she said immediately, 'You are English, I believe.'

'Yes.'

'We have already been informed about you, and we are quite satisfied.'

It was on the tip of my tongue to ask who had informed her, but thought better of it and remained silent. We entered into a comfortably furnished sitting room, where another middle-aged lady was sitting, knitting. She motioned us to be seated and our hostess said

'You may call me Flore, and this is my friend Annette.' Annette laid down her knitting and spoke

'Hello,' she said, in perfect English. 'How are you?'

Madame Flore smiled at our reaction of surprise.

'Yes, I am English,' continued Annette, 'but very few people around here know it. The Germans certainly do not. My husband is French, however, and works in Limoges. Flore and I learned of your necessary retreat from the hotel in Libourne, and you were fortunate that your guide had friends nearby who were prepared to help.'

How all this information had permeated through to these two ladies in Bergerac during the short time we had been in the area, we couldn't guess, nor did we ask.

'You will be quite safe here,' she said. 'Later this evening a man called Pierre will call to tell you what you have to do to cross the line.'

A small, cold midday meal was prepared during the course of which we learned we were not the first to have passed through this house and across the demarcation line, the most recent ones being three Americans. Prior to that, a number of army personnel left back after Dunkirk had turned up at various periods, and were helped to cross, en route for Marseilles and the Mediterranean coast were out and Toulouse was the focal gathering point. We were given a hotel address in Toulouse, where we would be put in touch with O'Leary. Again, the name O'Leary. He seemed to be known by everyone, and I was most curious and full of anticipation to meet this almost legendary man.

In the evening Pierre duly arrived, a cheerful youth of sixteen or seventeen, who worked at a farm a few kilometres distant to which he would take us tomorrow. In the meantime he was to show us an hotel where we would stay overnight.

'Do you have any money,' asked Annette, 'to pay for staying at the hotel and the train fare to Toulouse?'

'Yes, I believe we have sufficient between us.'

'Tomorrow,' the boy said, 'I will meet you outside the hotel and we will obtain bicycles and cycle together to the farm where I work.'

He gave us a time and told us to be ready promptly. Annette again spoke

'When you get across the Line, make for Monpazier, by bus. You will be able to get a train from there to Toulouse.'

Pierre then indicated that it was time to leave for the hotel, and after saying goodbye and voicing thanks to our two virtually unknown helpers, we accompanied the boy into the town.

The streets were alive with men in uniform, German Control Police, Wehrmacht and French Gendarmes, but we passed without incident. Pierre brought us to the hotel, reminded us of our instructions for morning and departed after giving us a small knapsack containing a little food and wine.

Entering the reception, which, like many similar French hotels, also contained a small bar. We saw the bar area thronged mainly with Germans of officer class, some drinking, others simply lounging and sitting talking or reading. No doubt it was out of bounds to other ranks, who would spend their leisure time in the numerous bistros and cafés.

To say that we were apprehensive would only be a mild description of our feelings, as we threaded our way through the groups of field grey uniforms towards the reception desk. I felt so frighteningly vulnerable, and, trying with concentrated effort to look unconcerned and natural, I would, to a close observer, have looked most unnatural, I'm certain. But we weren't subjected to close observation, that is, until we reached the desk.

The receptionist, a heavily bearded and moustached person, was intently watching our approach, and as we reached the desk he cast a quick glance around the uniformed company, as Eddy asked if we could have a room for the night.

'*Mais oui*,' he answered. 'It is already arranged, please sign the register,' and pushed it towards us.

We signed as per our false identity cards which we laid open in front of him, and at which he only gave a cursory glance, before handing them back to us. He gave us the number of the room, which was located on the top floor, and told us to use the stairs, because the lift did not go beyond the third floor, to save power. Behind his large moustache, I felt I detected a knowing grin as he wished us goodnight. We tramped upstairs, found our room, shutting and locking the door with a sense of considerable relief. There were twin beds onto which we gratefully sank.

'That was something of an effort,' remarked Eddy.

'What was?'

'Pushing through that crowd of Huns down there,' he said. 'Don't tell me you weren't scared!'

'Scared! I was petrified. The only thing I was conscious of was that bloke behind the desk. Did you see the way he was watching us? He knew who we were, you know. He'd been primed to expect us. Someone seems to be doing a lot of homework on our account.'

'Hope it stays that way,' replied Eddy. 'Let's get some shut-eye. It might be a heavy day tomorrow.'

We had breakfast in the bedroom, brought up by a chambermaid, and when we ventured down stairs, there was no sign of any Germans anywhere in the reception. There was a different receptionist who accepted payment for the room without comment and we left the hotel to see Pierre, across the road, gazing into a shop window. He moved away, and we followed him through side streets to a lock-up garage into which he entered, and produced two somewhat dilapidated bikes. We rode out of the town, a distance of about ten kilometres to the farm where he was employed part-time. The demarcation line actually passed through a vineyard behind the farm, and which was part of the estate.

Pierre introduced us to the owners of the farm who were obviously aware of what was afoot, and were genuinely happy at being involved. The bicycles were left in an outhouse and the boy went off on his own to reconnoitre and observe the passage of the patrol. After a while he returned.

'We are off,' he said briefly.

We followed him out of the house, accompanied by the owners of the farm, through the yard, to a gate which led on to the many tracks between the rows of vines, which, at this time of year, were quite bare. We passed slowly along sometimes stooping to examine the growth of the plants, as though we were visitors or friends being shown the vines. Pierre had noted the time of the passage of the patrol through the yard and knew they would not return until a certain time later. He was quite confident and satisfied that our progress through the vines, and across the invisible line would be accomplished in safety.

Presently he said, 'We are over.'

To us, the ground, the vines, the path appeared no different from any other part of the vineyard, and we continued on until we reached the far side where there was a border of high dense hedgerows and here, we relaxed and breathed more freely again. The farm couple shook hands and set off back through the vines to the house. The patrol had still not returned, and, of course had seen nothing.

Pierre motioned us to follow him along the far side of the hedge and we soon arrived at a narrow road, where was parked a small grey van, gaz-propelled, since a large cylinder type contraption occupied the roof.

Pierre then explained that the driver, a boy about the same age as himself, would take us to Monpazier railway station, where he would leave us. We had been told that to get to the station we would go by bus. This unexpected change of plan was most welcome. Seeing us safely into the back of the van, he bade us *bon voyage* and good luck and disappeared back along the hedge presumably to the farm and his work.

We never saw him again. Just another unknown French patriot, one of many other unknowns encountered during our eventful travels through France.

The driver let in the clutch and we were on our way.

CHAPTER TEN

Pat O'Leary

The journey to the station took about three-quarters of an hour through extremely pleasant country. Had it been peacetime, as tourists, the short car journey and subsequent train journey to Toulouse would have been a joy to behold. This part of France, Gascony and the Dordogne with its rolling countryside, winding steep-banked rivers and extensive vineyards is, I reckon, one of the loveliest areas of the country. We did, to a lesser degree, appreciate some of the scenery, even at this time of the year, but our minds were mainly occupied with more serious cogitations, than the beauty of the countryside. We clambered out of the little van which the driver had discreetly positioned behind a French Army personnel carrier in a far corner of the station yard. The last I saw of him he was disappearing into the buffet.

We bought two third-class tickets to Toulouse, entered to the platform and sat on a bench in the winter sunshine waiting for the train. The platform was crowded and I remarked to Eddy that we might be in for an uncomfortable ride. Nor was I wrong because when the train did arrive, there was a mad dash to get aboard. We had trouble keeping together, and when we finally did make it, found there were no seats vacant, and were obliged to stand in the corridor. The corridor itself was full of travellers, and Eddy found himself standing more or less shoulder to shoulder with a large gendarme who persisted in trying to make conversation. He soon gave it up when all he managed to receive in reply were muttered grunts, yawns and an occasional '*oui*' and '*non*'.

Further down the corridor I noticed another young man in a dark blue or black uniform, knee boots and breeches. His face was very pale and even at a distance his eyes were noticeably a pale blue, and intensely penetrating. I surmised, from what we were told, that this would be a member of the Vichy Milice, and someone to be avoided at all costs. I wouldn't like to have been confronted by that young man, and fervently hoped we could keep our distance when we reached Toulouse. Fortunately, he alighted at Montauban, but I realised that there would probably be many more like him in Toulouse. At Montauban we managed to obtain seats for the remainder of the journey.

Alighting at Toulouse, we mixed with the crowd to pass through the ticket barrier, and noted a distinct slowing up of movement. Two gendarmes in khaki uniform were examining papers. We were going to learn how good or bad our forged identity cards were.

As we got nearer, it was evident that the two Frenchmen had very little enthusiasm for the job they were doing, and their check was very desultory and haphazard. Many people presenting their cards were totally ignored or just given a cursory glance and waved on with impatient gestures. We passed through the barriers, in the latter category. I was of the opinion that we could have got through that control with a No. 9 London bus ticket. The gendarmerie of previously unoccupied France clearly didn't have their hearts in the job.

Toulouse is quite a large city, and consequently had a large station. Emerging from the platform, into a spacious concourse, alive with people, French and German, we noticed, in the centre, a large glass covered board with the title 'Information'. We made for this, and found what we had hoped for, a street map of the city. We were quickly able to locate the street, in which we had been told there was a small hotel, where we would obtain information on how to contact O'Leary.

The street was not far distant, and we found the hotel without trouble. We had been told to look out for a young, dark-haired hotel porter, who displayed a slight limp, the result of a war wound, and at an opportune moment, when there was no one near, speak to him, in English, telling him exactly who we were and could he help us.

The porter was not difficult to recognise and, although neither of us was entirely exhilarated about approaching a complete stranger, and openly declaring that we were RAF servicemen on the run, we did as instructed, as soon as it was practical. He registered a faint look of surprise, as though caught off guard, but quickly relaxed and gestured that we should return to the entrance of the hotel. Here he made a great show of giving the impression that he was giving us directions to find our way in the city, but in fact was telling us to go round to the rear of the hotel, where he had a little room of his own, and he would meet us there as soon as he could.

It was now quite dark, and we didn't meet or see anyone in the narrow street behind the hotel, whilst waiting for the porter to appear, and it wasn't long before he beckoned us into his little room which appeared to be an off-duty rest room containing a little cooker and wash basin. He offered us coffee, which we both accepted and, as we drank, he questioned us closely about how we managed to arrive at the hotel and who had told us about him. He spoke quite good English.

Without omitting anything, we told him of our arrival at Libourne, the events leading up to our crossing of the demarcation line and eventual arrival at Toulouse.

'*Eh bien!*' he exclaimed. 'In two hours my duty is done until tomorrow. Wait here, you will be quite safe, then you will come with me to see Monsieur Pat. He will require you to satisfy him completely on all points regarding identities.' He then left us to attend to his duties.

Well, I thought, is this the beginning of the last leg? Courage, determination and wit on the part of our French helpers, coupled with unbelievable luck on our part, had got us this far. Would we be permitted to succeed on this final stage? It seemed also, that at last we were to meet this chief of the escape line, the legendary 'Pat'.

The porter duly returned at the finish of his duty and accompanied us through a maze of unfrequented side streets and soon we arrived at what appeared to be a terrace of tall apartment blocks. Our porter friend spoke briefly to the concierge and we followed him upstairs to the third floor which consisted of quite a small landing with a couple of doors and a short corridor which ended in a window. It was lit by one electric light bulb, without a shade, and the floor, like the last flight of stairs, was uncarpeted. In all a very spartan and cheerless sort of place. There was an unmistakable hum of conversation coming from behind one of the doors, and it was into this room our guide ushered us.

The room was considerably larger than I expected, considering the size of the landing, and it too was very bare-looking. Against three of the walls, were some double tier bunks, with a various assortment of bedding. In the centre was a wooden table and three chairs. In a corner were dumped one or two small knapsacks whilst one or two more were hanging on the ends of the bunks. Some of the bunks and two of the chairs were occupied by a number of young men, most of whom eyed us curiously and silently as we entered.

I can't say why, but before the silence was broken, I realised that here were motley of chaps exactly like Eddy and me – on the run. Dressed as they were, some in a variety of ill-fitting suits, others in pullovers or cardigans, one with plus fours, I couldn't help conjuring up an impression of a fancy dress party, and it didn't occur to us, at the time, that we probably looked just as ridiculous. These chaps, like us, had been passed through France for varying periods of time, and accepted by all and sundry, friends or enemies alike, dressed as they were, but, coming face to face with their own countrymen, the guise was pretty threadbare. After all, it takes an accomplished actor to personify a character remote from himself, with a full degree of success.

A voice suddenly cried, 'Well, hello, two more candidates for the grand tour, I think!'

We were then subjected to a barrage of questions from everyone. How long have you been on the run? Where were you shot down? Fighter or Bomber Command? What kind of kite? Was it fighter or flak? Then came an exchange of Christian names and home towns which resulted in our learning that four of the chaps were Americans, survivors of a Fortress crew, brought down on a daylight raid near Aachen. The remainder were all English and included a Wing Commander fighter pilot shot down near Amiens on 10 December, four days after our debacle.

We learned that Toulouse was a rendezvous or collecting point, mainly for escaping and evading aircrew, but also for other servicemen and refugees, to make the mountain crossing into Spain, and 'Pat' had his HQ somewhere in the city. One or two blokes had been hidden here for just over two weeks, others for only a few days, but in a day or two it was hoped a party would leave for the frontier.

During this initial introduction and discussion, O'Leary himself joined us but never introduced himself by name. He was a young man of about thirty years, with sparse blond hair, fairly tall and with an authoritative disposition. Formerly he had been a doctor in a Belgian cavalry regiment, escaped to Britain and became an officer in the Royal Navy as a lieutenant-commander, where he assumed his clandestine name. His real name was Albert Marie-Guérisse.

Later he was captured in a small boat when attempting to rescue Polish airmen from the French Coast, just north of the Spanish border. He escaped from gaol, and was responsible for building and running an escape line first set up in late 1940 in Marseilles by Captain Ian Garrow, which linked up to the north of France and took its parcels out either by sea or over the Eastern Pyrenees.

In March 1943, only a month after our eventual departure from Toulouse, Pat was betrayed to the Gestapo by one of his recently acquired agents, suffered two years' imprisonment with constant torture, and was liberated from Dachau concentration camp in April 1945.

One of his chief lieutenants was an Australian girl Nancy Wake, married to a Frenchman since 1939. Quite accidentally she had become involved in helping servicemen to get out of Vichy France in 1941. As a result of her activities she became associated with O'Leary in Marseilles, until suspicion began to fall upon her from the Milice and Gestapo, necessitating a number of attempts to get out of France. She succeeded very soon after O'Leary's arrest and, after a training period in England, returned to France in 1944 to help organise the Resistance. These then were the people in whose hands we now were.

'You are the two new arrivals?' he enquired. We nodded. He turned and left the room abruptly. In a minute or two another man entered the room, and in French said O'Leary wanted to see us in another room, separately. I elected to go first, and followed the Frenchman out, and in to another room off the landing. It was a smaller room and there were three men seated on chairs behind the table, and a girl. One of the men was O'Leary. A single chair stood in front of the table. None of them got up and O'Leary indicated the chair and told me to sit down.

'You speak French?' he asked.

'Very badly,' I replied, 'but –'

'Never mind, we'll talk in English. What is your name?'

'Robertson – Henry.'

'Rank?'

'Sergeant, Royal Air Force.'

'Your friend's name?'

'Canter – Herbert.'

'Rank?'

'Same as me, sergeant RAF.'

'How old is he?'

'I'm not sure, slightly older than me, I think.'

'And you?'

'Twenty-seven.'

'What is your function in the crew?'

'Wireless operator.'

'And Canter?'

'Navigator.'

'When were you shot down, and where?'

'December 6, near Bar-le-Duc.'

'How?'

'German night fighters.'

'You were both in the same aircraft?'

'Yes.'

'What kind of aircraft?'

'Halifax.'

'Were you wounded when you were shot down?'

'No!'

'And you baled out?'

'Yes.'

'What happened to the rest of the crew?'

'I was told by a Frenchman that the pilot and rear gunner had been killed. I don't know what happened to the other three.'

'Good, you've done well to have got this far.'

'Thanks to a lot of brave people, and a good deal of luck,' I said.

One of the men got up and walked around towards my chair and offered me a cigarette. I accepted and the man proffered a light. He suddenly thrust his face close to mine and shouted something I couldn't understand. I stood up, casting an amazed look over the man's shoulder towards O'Leary, and then sat down again.

'What the hell does that mean?' I demanded.

'*C'est bon*,' said the man, and the others round the table were laughing.

'We expected you to react in your own language, and you did,' said O'Leary. 'You may leave and please send in your friend.'

O'Leary and his team were evidently quite satisfied as to our bona fides, because Eddy wasn't subjected to a similar procedure.

We slept on mattresses on the floor of the adjacent room and in the morning breakfasted very simply with the rest of the chaps in their accommodation. Later some articles of clothing and stout shoes were brought us to sort out for wearing on the mountain journey.

Nothing transpired that day, nor the next, until evening when Nancy, the Australian girl, informed us that it would be probable that we would leave the next day. The hold-up had been due to the difficulty in hiring mountain guides. This had now been arranged.

That same evening two more bodies joined us, one a fighter pilot of Belgian origin but flying with the RAF, whilst the other, remarkably enough, was a British army corporal, left back after Dunkirk, had been on the loose ever since, and completed 'a grand tour of France' as he jokingly described it. He was still wearing his khaki slacks under a pair of baggy French trousers and his army boots which proved invaluable.

We left the apartment block in ones and twos, and at intervals, the next morning, meeting up again in Toulouse railway station. At the station another three chaps latched on to the party. They had been holed up in a hotel the previous night, where O'Leary had screened them for security. O'Leary and two young Frenchmen escorted us in groups to the station, where they purchased tickets for various destinations en route to Aix-les-Thermes, but instructed us that we would all leave the train at a place called Ussat. One of the young Frenchmen was to accompany us to Ussat, where, it was hoped, the Spanish guides would take over, upon receiving payment from him.

During our short stay in Toulouse we had plenty of time to talk to our new companions and learned that they had been evading for various periods of time, ranging from three to six months, and in most cases, had been the victims of night fighters, like ourselves. One or two had suffered such severe damage over their targets, that they were forced to abandon their aircraft on the way back or crash-land. All had been helped on their way by patriotic French people or minor resistance groups, but none, it would appear, had experienced the superb treatment and luck that had befallen us. The Americans, in particular, had had a pretty rough time, one still suffering from a bullet wound, received when he escaped from a German patrol into which he had unexpectedly run after baling out.

We were surreptitiously handed our tickets by O'Leary and his aides, and split up into ones and twos so as not to be too conspicuous as a crowd, and eventually boarded the train in the same manner. Unlike on our previous train journeys, this train was not crowded at all, and we were able to spread ourselves out into various compartments and travel in relative comfort. It was fortunate that no security check was made en route, because we learned later, that one or two chaps had not been provided with French identity cards or travel permits. It would have been really tough luck if they had been pulled off the train at this stage, after having got so far.

So we were on our way, every one of us surely and fervently hoping that this was to be the final and successful stage of our eventful journey through enemy occupied territory.

After a journey of just under two hours we arrived and alighted from the train at Ussat. It was now beginning to get dark and we exited from the platform where there was no control, into what seemed to be merely a wayside halt, which hardly warranted a train stop. It was, in fact, a very, very small community in the Pyrenean foothills, and we didn't remain long enough to see anything of it. The two guides were awaiting our arrival and they and our young courier conversed together for a short while, during which a package was exchanged, being no doubt the payment for services rendered. The Frenchman bade us farewell with a reassurance that we were in capable hands and, with luck, would be over the frontier by the following day.

The guides generally were Spanish, men who, before the war, had earned their living entirely as smugglers. Then it had been contraband goods, now the contraband was supplemented by bodies, live ones, of course. They were wanted in Spain by the Franco regime for various crimes, sometimes including murder, and of course smuggling, whilst in France the Gestapo were after them. It was therefore in their interests to keep moving over the frontier, never remaining long on either side. They were both a cut-throat looking couple, but we were to learn that they knew their job – and their mountains thoroughly. The one who appeared to be the senior was a swarthy young man, about thirty years old, wiry and slim with an enormous shock of black hair. His companion, also with a well weathered, swarthy complexion, was a bull of a man, who showed a wide toothy grin, when he chose.

We walked in the darkness for about one and a half hours and spent the rest of the night in a barn. Here the guides produced pairs of rope-soled espadrilles which they said were better for rock climbing and were much quieter when marching along the rocky tracks. These tracks had been specially selected because of their remoteness from German patrol routes, by virtue of their very high altitude and extreme roughness. I preferred to wear the boots originally given me by Fernand.

The usual escape routes over the Pyrenees at this period were either near the west coast, via the Biarritz area, or via Perpignan in the east. These were heavily guarded and patrolled. Our guides therefore proposed to cross between these two areas, into the little Republic of Andorra and thence into Spain. It would be a very strenuous journey over a very high section of the mountains, they told us, sometimes dangerous, but on the other hand, with less likelihood of encountering German patrols. They added, that they had used the route many times, before the war. One aspect which they failed to take into consideration however, was the appalling weather conditions at this time of the year, and these were to cost our party dearly. The winter of 1942-1943 was extremely severe in Britain, let alone in the Central Pyrenees.

We were awakened in the morning by the two guides, who took us a few hundred yards up a road behind the barn and arrived at a farm where coffee and bread had been provided for us, presumably arranged either by the guides of the young French courier of the previous day.

The two guides were dressed ready for the off. They both had woollen hats pulled well down over their ears, heavy woollen jackets and rope soled shoes. The slimmer of the two carried a pack on his back, and a long shafted ice-axe, slung from his wrist. I noticed also that each carried a gun under their woollen jackets.

Soon they indicated that it was time to go and we finished off the coffee, followed them into the open, and set off walking at a reasonable pace, which we soon realised was a challenge to us to keep in contact with the person in front. One guide preceded the little column, the other brought up the rear, a tactic which we were to learn was not without purpose. We had been warned that the guides tended to keep going and were very disinclined to stop for stragglers.

It was a beautiful morning, the sun just beginning to give a little warmth out of a deep blue cloudless sky. I knew, however, how quickly weather can change in mountainous country. Personally, I was looking forward to the trek over the mountains, since my favourite hobby and activity at home was extensive rock climbing and fell walking, mainly in the English Lake District. I knew, nevertheless, that this mountain passage was undoubtedly going to be something of a more taxing nature than the Fairfield Horseshoe or the Newlands Round in Cumbria. Brief glimpses of lofty snow-covered, serrated or jagged peaks projecting into the sky were, to me, a magnet, first because the other side spelled freedom, secondly because I felt in my element. To all but a minority in the party, the sight of these formidable turrets was very daunting. Eddy, for one, was definitely discouraged, judging by some of his muttered remarks.

We marched and climbed with a ten minute rest every two hours. The guides were implacable about this, and I guess they were right, because it resulted in a sort of rhythm being attained.

Walking and climbing through the foothills, trees got smaller and scantier until the track broke out into open rough country, littered with boulders, and with fast running streams racing down to the valleys. Before leaving the trees behind, the guides had us cut robust branches to use as walking aids initially, and perhaps as a more effective aid, later. They themselves helped in this task.

As we climbed higher, so the air became colder and thinner and we saw the first traces of snow. A wind was now getting up, blowing from our right, the north-west, and a few clouds also began to appear from the same direction. Conversation became less and less, as the going became more difficult, but the pace never lessened. The path or track lost itself in areas of limestone and scree, and far ahead, the ragged, serrated dragon's teeth of the Pyrenees began to assume menacing proportions.

By mid afternoon, most of us were puffing and blowing as we strove to keep up the relentless pace being set by the Spaniard in front, whilst being constantly chivied by his companion in the rear. It needed compulsive concentration, and determination, to keep contact with the man in front, and at times became a scramble. The wind had by now become much stronger and the sinking sun was being obscured by thick cloud banks.

Ahead, at right angles to the track, we saw a kind of rock step, only three or four feet high, but extending to left and right, as far as the eye could see. Here the guides stopped saying that we could enjoy a longer rest, and eat. We squatted into crevices in the rock step, sheltering from the wind and bread and cheese was produced from the pack carried by the slim young guide whose name we learned was Juan. We were allowed a mouthful of wine from the goatskin bags and two sugar lumps each.

As we rested and ate, Juan took stock of the situation and noting that one or two of us were in a rather distressed condition, gave warning that if anyone had doubts about being able to proceed, now was the time to say so and turn back, because the going was likely to worsen as we got higher. The weather too, was showing signs of deterioration and could complicate the situation further. Weakness on anyone's part could endanger other members of the party, and jeopardise chances of success. The American who had been wounded admitted that he was already feeling the effects of the strenuous climb, and the cold, and was prepared to return to Ussat, hoping to recover enough to join a later party. He didn't look in any fit state to return on his own and the Belgian pilot gallantly offered to go back with him to ensure his safety.

The sun had, by now, disappeared and darkness fell swiftly as the dejected couple bade us goodbye and good luck, and began retracing the track down to the valley. Many times since, I've wondered how they fared. Did they get down successfully, and, if they did, was a second successful attempt made on a subsequent occasion? I like to think that they eventually made it, particularly the Belgian. He, of all people, deserved to be compensated for his unselfish actions, which he knew would rob him of his chance on this particular venture.

The rest of us continued our march and we began to encounter much deeper snow, whilst the temperature dropped alarmingly. The next time we halted, after the usual two hour trek, it began to snow, the wind rose and soon we were being lashed by a biting blizzard. The two guides at this stage began conferring with one another and were clearly worried. They seemed to be fairly certain of our position because, as a result of their deliberations, they said that a little further on there should be a hut and we would spend the rest of the evening and night there, hoping the storm would abate. It took a lot of willpower to set us all on the move again, and the concentrated effort of steep uphill climbing tended to help us ignore the frightening conditions around us, and, in addition, kept our blood circulation flowing.

Both guides were out in front now, partly, I suppose, because two heads and four eyes had more chance of locating the hut they were looking for, and partly to help our passage by kicking steps and treading a track through the deepening snow. It was difficult to compare the present nightmarish conditions with the weather as it had existed when we had started off that morning. My experience of peacetime fell walking had taught me how weather conditions can violently and abruptly change in mountainous country, but I hadn't experienced anything even remotely resembling this fantastic and frightening state of affairs.

Suddenly, from ahead, out of the darkness the voice of one of our guides signalled their arrival at the mountain hut, and one by one we plodded up to join them in the small shelter. Built of wood on a low foundation of rocks, it was devoid of anything in the way of furniture, but round the inner walls was a rough kind of bench. It was probably used by mountain shepherds, although the only trace of previous occupation was a storm lantern suspended from a roof beam and, luckily, the guides discovered that it contained some oil.

CHAPTER ELEVEN

Disaster in the Pyrenees

It was sheer bliss to be out of the icy wind and snow and we thankfully sank down on to the bench seat. Even the two guides seemed relieved to get out of the blizzard, but they busied themselves tearing up some of the seating, hacking some of it into thin slivers with the ice axes and tried to coax a fire. It was extremely difficult without paper tinder but in due course they succeeded.

We must have looked a sorry lot, and gazing round, I was relieved to see that Eddy looked OK, obviously pretty exhausted, but not unduly worried. The Wingco pilot looked to be in good shape too, as did four of the others including the army corporal. The fire had soon a good hold, but since there was no chimney the door had to be left open, to get rid of the smoke, at the same time letting in draughts of freezing air and snow. Nevertheless, we appreciated the warmth, and the guides handed out some more bread and wine, more sugar lumps and, surprisingly, some dried prunes.

In spite of the discomfort and the racket of the wind, I nodded off and slept for two or three hours. When I awoke some of the others were asleep, and also one of the guides. Someone had evidently kept the fire going, the wind had dropped but it was snowing heavily.

The guides again conversed together finally deciding it was necessary to carry on when it became daylight, even though it was snowing, and so reach the head of the pass before nightfall.

We set off once more under a leaden sky and found walking much more difficult in the soft deep snow. At times we were thigh deep and had to literally crawl, using the tree branches, which we had cut previously, horizontally across our bodies with both hands, to prevent sinking chest deep. There was little time to dwell on any but our immediate problems, there was no future, we were embarked on a great change and were already beyond the point of no return. Seemingly, ages ago, all our cares in the outer world had been concerned with very trivial things of life, now our first concern was to concentrate on putting one leg in front of the other, lean hard on the horizontal branch, and drag the other leg out from behind to continue the process. The temperature must have been well below zero, but our efforts often were such as to cause us to sweat freely, until, during the brief halts, we rapidly cooled and began to freeze. We were living on a knife edge, crossing, not just a frontier on a map, but into an unknown and untried part of ourselves. I distinctly remember a moment when I thought a humble mug of NAAFI tea would represent the very peak of human happiness.

We began to descend a gradual slope, and the ground became firmer, so firm in fact that we began to slide until we reached a sort of arena ringed by high peaks, and the guides said it was a frozen lake. Normally they skirted this large sheet of water, to climb the high pass on the other side. This time they took a direct route, straight across the ice. We followed, slipping, sliding and sometimes falling, to reach the other side.

As we commenced the climb, the wind rose again, and once more we were lashed with a raging blizzard as we kicked and hacked steps up the ice covered cliff. One of the Americans cried out that they must halt, he could go no further, but the guides would have none of it, and pressed on. Looking back, I saw the American collapse on the steep slope and begin sliding back, and someone else stopping to go after him and assist. Still the guides would not wait, insisting we reach the summit of the track.

But finally, it ended. We struggled the last few feet to the crest and crowded together under a snow-covered rock overhang, none of us now believing that we would ever reach Spain. The guides were themselves nearly exhausted but, after a more lengthy rest, started digging and scraping a snow cave under the overhang. The wind started to abate, it stopped snowing and suddenly there was a moon, not full, but full enough to reveal the ghostly terrain around us. We had a little more bread and wine and the guides set off down the tracks we had made during the ascent to find the two Americans. They returned nearly two hours later, practically dragging one of them up the slope; the other, they said, was dead. That night the other one died also, most certainly of exhaustion and exposure. He was also badly frost-bitten.

The night was spent in the snow cave, under the overhang, but no one slept. If we had, we wouldn't have awakened, and we kept the blood circulating as best we could. Both guides admitted that never before had they experienced such appalling conditions. In good weather they could make the crossing in eight or nine hours. Up to now, we had been on the go for over two days, but the worst was over, only one more pass, and then the final descent into Andorra. The body of the American was left in the snow cave under the overhang.

We started off again before sunrise, with the remaining American now complaining of severe pain in his feet, and one or two of the others quite obviously had varying degrees of frostbite. On one occasion we were forced to traverse the shoulder of a steep snow-covered slope in order to avoid an area of grim-looking ice pinnacles, forming a glacier covering the route up the pass. Suddenly there was a sound of heavy surf beating against a rocky headland, and great clouds of spindrift came hissing over. The snow under our feet began to move, en masse, taking some of us with it. At this point the leading guide was slightly below us, and we saw him begin to slide as he shouted: 'Avalanche!'

He rolled over and face down, holding his ice axe close to his chest, dug the blade into the snow to act as a brake. The snow was too loose to hold the blade and too deep, and he disappeared into the moving mass along with two of the party who were immediately behind him. Some of us, including myself, were fortunate enough to maintain an upright stance, as we were carried down, others were partially buried as the slide halted, and were able to extricate themselves. Of the guide there was no trace! The rear guide had escaped the moving platform of snow, and quickly joined us, frantically digging into the snow using hands and feet, in an effort to locate his companion. As we kicked and clawed away at the snow, there was always the danger of another movement taking place, but luckily we were spared that possible disaster, and to our relief we soon had him out, shaken and shocked, but otherwise unhurt, and still clutching his axe.

We rested, where we were, until about midday and when the

gale had subsided, we started again along the traverse, under an almost clear sky, although now and again, great banks of mist blotted out the slopes ahead and around us. After one more stint of nearly two hours, we reached the crest of the final pass and were able to look, with an uninterrupted view, down into Andorra, lying far below us. Later, when studying a map of the area, we discovered that the height of the pass at that point was 2,900 metres, just under 10,000 feet.

The descent to the green fields and streams of the little Republic would be over very rough ground, we knew, but we were across the frontier, out of occupied France, with freedom within sight, or so we thought.

It took the rest of that day to reach the low ground and after numerous slitherings and stumblings and not a few minor falls, we reached valley bottom in darkness, and although it was still jolly cold, there was not a trace of snow. The majority of our little party, now numbering only eleven, were really suffering the effects of exhaustion, exposure and in a number of cases, frostbite. The two guides had orientated themselves, and assured us that very near there was a village where they were known to the inhabitants and we must press on – it would only take an hour, at the most. We struggled on determinedly, and in less than an hour, the lights of the village appeared through the darkness ahead, and soon we stumbled into a narrow cobblestone street and followed the two Spaniards into a low-roofed, stone built cottage.

Three things indelibly impressed themselves on my mind on entering the cottage. First, the enormity of the room into which we found ourselves; secondly, the unbelievable, but welcome, hot atmosphere; and thirdly, oddly enough, the sight of an enormous pile of dark brown leaves heaped against one wall (they turned out to be tobacco leaf). To me, anyway, these three first impressions, strange as they might appear, given normal circumstances, were like a transition from our arctic hell to a comforting equatorial heaven. The heat emanated from the largest open fire I had ever seen, around which were an assortment of cooking pots and utensils.

The occupants, a middle-aged couple, were evidently well known to our two guides since the greetings were unquestionably enthusiastic, although we couldn't understand the voluble exchanges of Spanish. The gestures and expressions, however, left no doubt in my mind that the guides were elaborating on the frightful events of the past three days. The younger guide explained to us later, that they had told of the deaths of the two Americans and assured us that, when the weather improved, the bodies would be recovered. I like to think that this was accomplished, but we never learned anything or heard any more about the disaster.

We were given food and drink, sitting on the floor against the room walls, and very soon fell asleep in that position, overcome by fatigue and the overpowering heat after all the hours of severe cold. In the morning we were examined by someone who professed to be something of a medic, and as a result, the remaining Americans and six others of the party were taken to either a doctor's surgery or small hospital for attention to severe frostbite. The American, we understood, would probably lose a foot. This left Eddy, the wing commander, the army corporal and myself, the only four members to be in any state of fitness for the remainder of the journey into Spain itself, which would involve another mountain journey, not of such severity or duration however.

Together with our two guides, we left the village, Canillo was its name, to stay one day at a small hotel near the capital, Andorra-la-Vierja.

I can only presume that the chaps left back in Andorra did manage to get into Spain and eventually back to England after recovering. I cannot be certain, but hope that they did.

The reason for our emergence from the ordeal with surprising fitness I can only think was attributable to the luck we had in meeting the people we did during our passage through France. The way we had been looked after and fed by these courageous people, had undoubtedly kept us physically fit and more able to withstand the rough mountain crossing. A further, and more spiritual aspect can, perhaps, also be taken into consideration. When we left Ruffec for our second sojourn in Paris, and our forthcoming journey over the Pyrenees, Madame Denivelle presented each of us with a Lourdes medallion, and the verbal assurance, that its possession would guarantee us 'a safe journey home'. I still possess the medallion, and continue to visit Madame Denivelle in Ruffec, and apart from severe arthritis, she continues to enjoy good health.

Having spent a comfortable night in the hotel and partaken

of a larger than usual breakfast, the two guides and the four of us left the little capital to make our way across the remaining mountain barrier into Spain.

As we climbed out of the lowlands, we again reached the snowline, but encountered none of the difficulties previously experienced, and by early evening had descended the foothills into Spain. Here the guides skilfully avoiding the Spanish border guards, took us to a small inn, where we enjoyed our first real meal for days – some kind of meat with batter of egg, flour and breadcrumbs, deep-fried in oil and garnished. The last meal comparable with this, enjoyed by Eddy and me, had been at Madame Denivelle's in Ruffec a month or two previously.

That evening Juan, the younger guide, explained that we would be obliged to remain at the inn for a day or two whilst he went ahead into Barcelona to inform the British Consul of our arrival in neutral Spain. In the meantime, to avoid police activity in the frontier regions, we would spend the nights in a nearby barn, rather than in the inn, so once more we spent our sleeping hours in the hay. During the day we were safely hidden in a farmhouse which was just as well, because early one morning a squad of Spanish police – suspecting the innkeeper of hoarding produce and hiding contraband goods – chose to swoop on the inn. From our concealment in the farm, we were able to observe them entering the inn, some in their medieval three-cornered black hats, and eventually departing, after an unsuccessful search.

The sight of these uniformed Spanish Civil Guards reminded us that we were not yet entirely out of the wood. We learned that some evaders had successfully arrived in Spain, only to be arrested by the police on the charge of illegal entry, and found themselves as prisoners in either one of the Spanish internment camps of Miranda or Figueras, where they would spend varying periods of internment, before arrangements through diplomatic channels effected their release.

After Juan's departure for Barcelona, supposedly to acquaint the Consul of our whereabouts, I was constantly beset by the doubt that perhaps he wouldn't return. After all, the guides were normally paid half their fees by the Resistance leaders in France and received the other half from the British authorities in Spain, after successfully delivering their charges. Even half the fee was a considerable amount, so would he be satisfied and not be unduly worried about the other half? I voiced my doubts to the others but, after discussion, we argued that, since he had left his companion with us during his absence, he probably had every intention of keeping his word and would return in due course. The fact that he had not actually returned by the second day after departure was disconcerting, but early on the morning of the third day, we were awakened from our slumbers in the barn, by the sound of a very English-sounding voice calling us to 'rise and shine' and upon coming awake, the first thing I saw was a twenty packet of Capstan cigarettes being waved about before my eyes.

We all agreed afterwards, it couldn't have seemed more like a pleasant dream, but it was a fact. Juan had returned, and with him was a senior official from the Consulate in Barcelona. Without any delay or preamble, we were bundled into a large saloon car and were on our way to Barcelona, where we arrived in the afternoon. The date was 18 February.

We remained until 27 February, at the residence of the Vice-Consul, and during our stay were given the opportunity to write to our people at home, and were taken to the Consulate where various documents had to be filled in and passport photographs taken. The forged French identity cards we had to surrender, and these were destroyed. We enjoyed the luxury of a haircut and were issued with quite smart civilian clothing. Finally we were each handed an Emergency Certificate, signed by the British Consulate General, and valid for the journey of a 'British subject to the United Kingdom'.

The following day we left by car bound for the British Embassy in Madrid where we were to be housed for a further seven days subsequent to which we travelled, by train, to La Linea, and were shuttled across the 'no man's land' dividing Spain from Gibraltar, in a mini-bus, in company with an odd assortment of other individuals who might have been either legitimate workers, refugees or perhaps more dubious characters.

Since arriving in Madrid we had seen no more of our wing commander companion, for whom alternative arrangements had presumably been made, and the three of us found ourselves once more subject to service regulations on the Rock. Three days later, Gibraltar began slowly to fall behind, when we set sail in one of a large convoy of vessels bound for Britain. The seven day voyage was interrupted by constant alarms of potential U-boat attacks, and I admit to being more scared during that trip than at any time whilst dodging the Germans in France. In any case it would have been something of an anti-climax to be lost on the homeward sea journey, after the success of the past three months. The efforts of all our brave French helpers would have been in vain.

To minimise the possibility of attack in the Bay of Biscay, the convoy was routed via the Atlantic, up the West Coast of Ireland, south into the Irish Sea, and we docked safely at Liverpool on 14 March.

With minimum delay we entrained for London where we underwent a searching and methodical debriefing session at the Air Ministry, after which we were ordered to RAF Uxbridge for repatriation arrangements and re-kitting.

The situation at Uxbridge turned out to be rather amusing, in that we were billeted with a hutful of aircrew NCOs, destined to be AC2s the following day, as a result of being labelled LMF (lack of moral fibre). We were immediately assumed to be similar candidates for demotion and these unfortunate chaps took a lot of convincing that we had been on the run in occupied France since 6 December.

When asked what we would prefer to do, after a period of leave, we both opted to continue as air crew, but were told that we could no longer be allowed to take part in European bomber operations and I personally requested Coastal Command. My posting came through to me whilst on leave, and I found myself in Transport Command, where I was to remain until the end of the war.

I have no idea where Eddy went; I only saw him once more, very briefly, at Buckingham Palace for our investiture in December that year.

Through the RAF Escaping Society's Newsletter, I learned that he died in 1985.

We were lucky, there's no doubt about that. But it is as well to remember, at this stage, that Eddy and I were two, out of two and a half thousand successful RAF evaders, the majority of whom would never have achieved a home run, had it not been for the courage and resourcefulness of so many French men, women and youngsters, who at supreme risk to themselves, their families and friends, gave such invaluable help.

True, in France, as in many other occupied countries, there were people only too ready to collaborate with the Germans, betray their fellow countrymen and allies and commit treason, mainly for financial gain and easier living conditions. Fortunately these were in a small minority and subsequently paid the penalty for their disloyalty. The Mayor of Fresnes-au-Mont, the village where our three comrades were turned over to the Germans, mysteriously disappeared one day, and wasn't heard of again. Rough justice, no doubt.

I am glad I was there, proud to be able to say that I was one of those given such help and, to this day, value the friendship of those of my helpers who still survive.

Appendix A

In September 1986, 76 Squadron held their first reunion, and it has now become an annual event, held in York.

It was at this reunion that I met John Theckston, the mid-upper gunner from my aircraft, and whom I had not seen since we climbed into our aircraft at Linton-on-Ouse, on that fateful night of 6 December 1942.

Naturally we had plenty to talk about and were able to exchange the story of our individual experiences. John was one of the three crew members who spent three years as a POW. He told me that after landing he had met up with MacDonald and Parkin, the bomb aimer and flight engineer, and had set off walking through the forest, as I had done, but in a different direction. Parkin had a broken ankle and without medical attention stood very little chance of avoiding capture. Anyway they eventually arrived in the small village of Fresnes-au-Mont, were recognised as aircrew and taken to the house of the Mayor of the village. They were given something to eat, Parkin's ankle was inspected, and they assumed all was well until later in the day two German officers turned up, and they were arrested.

Apparently the Mayor was either an active collaborator or he was too scared to give further help and had informed the local German commander of the circumstances. They were taken to a guard room in Bar-le-Duc, pending transfer to a POW camp and were visited by the pilot of the night fighter who had shot us down. Theckston described him as a gentleman, certainly not of the usual Nazi breed, and he was anxious to know whether we had all landed without injury, after baling out. He spoke extremely good English and explained that he had had some education in England and thought it a wonderful country.

After his arrival in a prison camp in Poland, John was able to write to his father, indicating that he and two others were prisoners, and he assumed, the rest of the crew had baled out successfully and would probably turn up sooner or later. His father wrote to my people in a similar strain, thus providing the hope that I was still alive, which, in the event, proved to be so.

Appendix B

I explained in the text of a fairly recent visit to Monsieur Fernand Cherrier, who up till then had not visited or even knew of the exact spot where the aircraft crashed.

While we were visiting the cemetery of Courouvre, he got into conversation with a local farmer by the name of Louis Perignon, who remembered the incident well, and offered to take Fernand and myself to see the spot, which was not far distant from the village of Courouvre.

The following day we did this, and were conducted off the road into a small wood. Here a lot of trees had been cut down since the war, and re-afforestation had been and still was taking place using different types of trees.

The owner of the forest and the land had however, in a token of respect, left the area of impact just as it had been in 1942, and there remained the trunks of two very tall trees with the tops sheared off by the wings of the Halifax when it had ploughed into them. The area below, and in close proximity to the trees, was kept fairly free of subsequent undergrowth, and traces of burning could still be discerned where the aircraft had lain and burnt itself out.

It was quite a traumatic experience.

One of the villagers still had some lengths of parachute lines which had belonged to the rear gunner killed in the crash, and insisted that I take a small length home with me as memorabilia.

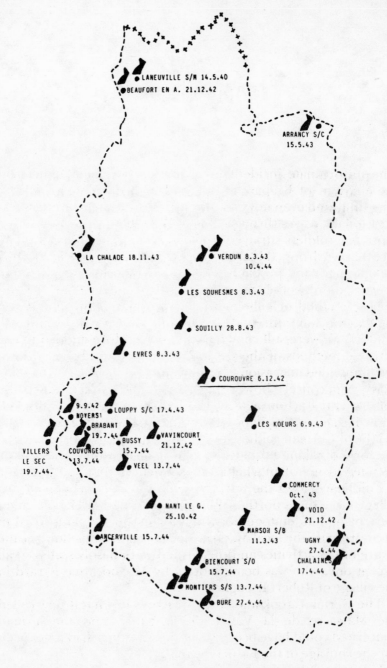

Allied aircraft shot down in the Meuse area of France 1939–1944.

Appendix C

The unfortunate incident involving two German soldiers on the environs of Brabant-le-Roi, had both of us worried for a long time, and even now, 44 years after the event, the awfulness occasionally passes through my mind. If I knew for certain that those two soldiers survived, I would be more than happy. The fact that we dropped bombs from 12,000 feet or less every time we operated, and probably killed many innocent people in the process, didn't bother most aircrews. It seemed a detached and remote method of killing. But man to man confrontation on the ground was entirely different and mentally disturbing. As evaders, we were still combatants and therefore entitled to use extreme methods, if the situation demanded it, but it was not recommended in evasion procedure.

My main concern however, both at the time and now, was the consequential action against the local population. It was well known that acts of sabotage or resistance, resulting in the deaths of German soldiers or agents, brought about revenge in the form of taking hostages in varying ratios, sometimes five or even ten to one, all of whom were summarily shot.

I did learn, after the war, that such reprisals were taken in a village some miles north of Revigny, where, in 1944, 25 airmen were being hidden together with a British agent parachuted in to co-ordinate the local Maquis. The Germans somehow became aware of the activities and the airmen were hastily scattered all except one, who was being hidden by M. and Mme Evrard in the village of Robert Espagne.

The Germans took and shot 85 victims in what is now called the Massacre de la Vallée de la Saulx, and the airman concerned could have been one of these victims, had it not been for the courage of the French couple.

I visited the location of our confrontation with the Germans, near Brabant-le-Roi, in May 1986, and after making enquiries among the residents of the village and with the present mayor, I was satisfied, and pleased, that there was no knowledge of any similar reprisal having been taken as the result of our action that night. Perhaps the two Germans survived after all.

Appendix D

In my narrative, I recounted how, after the incident in the village of Rancourt-sur-Ornain, we were given valuable assistance in the way of accommodation, food and transport to Vitry-le-François railway station and eventually to Paris. We never knew or found out the names of this family except for the man, Bernard, who took us to Vitry-le-François station, accompanied us to Paris, and led us to the Rue St Claude and Monsieur Roussel.

We learned from Odette that, a short while after the event, the Frenchman and his wife to whom we had mentioned Odette's name, visited Rancourt and called upon Odette and her father and explained that the two English flyers whom he had hidden on 12 December had been safely sent on their way accompanied to Paris, where, no doubt, they would be in the good hands of Odette's uncle. Odette was, of course, fully aware of what the man was talking about, but not being entirely sure of his identity and being suspicious that it could be a ruse on the part of the Gestapo to discover people who were giving help to shot-down airmen, denied all knowledge of the incident and sent the couple back to their home in the village of Heiltz, probably disgruntled and disappointed.

Such was the suspicion harboured, even among near neighbours, of possible German infiltration and the need for extreme care in both word and deed.

Later of course, Odette was to learn of the arrest, torture and death of this man, because of his many other activities and remained perpetually sorry that she was unable to accept his story, and celebrate the success of their joint efforts.

Many such French people helped us in all manner of ways, risking everything for nothing, except perhaps, the satisfaction of contributing towards the return of valuable fighting men to

England. There are few; a very few whom I know and have been able to thank. The majority were strangers; we met them, asked for help, were given it and we continued on our way. Others willingly hid us for a time and passed us on.

The poster drawn up by the occupying forces and exhibited in many French villages, towns and cities (see the photograph reproduced in this book) left no doubt in the minds of everyone, the penalties being risked for nothing, and in the process, the forfeiture of what would have been, for the ordinary French countryman or townsman, a small fortune. I shall be forever in their debt and cannot really express the gratitude felt towards these known and unknown, quite ordinary people. I refer to them as 'ordinary' because, the majority were in no escape line or underground movement and yet they contributed almost as much to the success of our evasion.

Index

Aachen, 21
Abwehr, 16
Aix-le-Thermes, 148
Alice Hawthorn pub, 23
Alps, 21
American Fortress survivors, 145, 149, 152, 155, 156
Ançelôt, Jean, curé of St Julien, 60, 61, 62
Andorra, 150
Angoulême, 106
Anson aircraft, 21

Barcelona, 159, 160
Bar-le-Duc, 35, 45, 65
Beachy Head, 32
Beatrice, 101
Beningboro Hall, 21
Bergerac, 128, 131
Berlin, 25
Bernadette, 96, 98, 99, 100
Bernard, 91
Betty's Bar, 22
Biarritz, 150
Blackpool Initial Training, 42
Bomber Command No 4 Group, 19
Bordeaux, 105, 115
Boulet, André, 109, 112
Boyle, Andrew, 19
Brabant-le-Roi, 62, 66, 67, 69, 74, 82
Brandy Zone Nord Line, 127
British Consul, 159

Canillo, 158
Canter, 'Eddy', 20, 21, 23, 31, 54

Cavell, Edith, 128
Chalôns-sur-Marne, 90
Charante, 106
Chardac, Yves, 97, 103, 104, 105, 106, 107, 119, 120, 121, 123
Chardogne, 66
Charles, 96, 103-7
Château, Thierry, 90
Cherrier, Fernard, 51-64
Cherrier, Mme, 57
Cheshire, Gp Capt Leonard, 19, 28, 38
Chesterfield, Lady, 21
Christmas Eve, 1942, 110-11
Cockleshell Heroes, 115
Cologne, 21
Commando survivors, 94
Commercy, 45
Convoy from Gibraltar, 161
Courouvre, 57, 165

Dachau concentration camp, 146
Demarcation line, 128
Denivelle, Gaston, 107
Denivelle, Max, 110, 112
Denivelle, Renée, 106, 158
Dordogne, 142
Dunkirk, 138, 148

Eighth Army, 92
Emergency certificate, 160
Emile, 126
Escape Kit, 19

Flensburg, 21
Flore and Annette, 138
Forêt de Koers, 50

Franco, General, 150
Frankfurt, 25
Fresnes-au-Mont village, 58, 162, 163

Gascony, 142
Genoa, 21
Georges, 126, 127, 130
Georgette, 50
Germaine, 102
German Freya Radar, 33
Gestapo, 16, 104
Gibraltar, 160
Grimaux, Monsieur, 109
Grimecourt, 45, 47
Guérisse, Lt Cdr Albert-Marie, see O'Leary, Pat

Halifax bomber, 19, 20, 22, 24, 27
Hasler, Major, 94
Hillier, P/O Bill, 20, 21, 23, 32, 34, 35, 40, 50
Hôtel de France, Ruffec, 119, 120
Hôtel de l'Orient, Libourne, 143
Hôtel les Toques Blanches, Ruffec, 116

IFF equipment, 24, 33
Internment camps, Spain, 159

Jacques, 130, 133-138
Juan, Spanish guide, 152, 159
Junkers 88 nightfighter, 34

Kiel, 21
Kinloss, OTU, 21, 37, 43
Krefeld, 21

Laimont, 66
La Linea, 160
Lancaster, 32
Lavallée village, 60, 68, 72
Leon, 113
Levoncourt, 50, 72
Libourne, 133

Limoges, 138
Lindell, Mary (Marie-Claire), 110, 115
Linton-on-Ouse, 19, 20, 43
Lorraine, 45
Lourdes medallion, 158
Luftwaffe pilot, 57
Lyons, 102
Lysander, 117, 118

McDonald, Sgt, 20
Madrid, 160
Magdeburg, 25
Mannhiem, 25, 33
Maquis, 109
Mario, 97
Mario (lawyer), 129
Marseilles, 146
Marston Moor, 22
Massacre de la Vallée de la Saulx, 167
Merlins, 34
Messerschmitt 110, 34
Middleton St George, 19, 20
Milice, 15, 16
Milleville, Comtesse de, see Lindell, Mary
Montmartre, 101
Montparnasse, 101

Newton-on-Ouse, 19
Nun Monkton, 43

Odette, 84, 88
O'Leary, Pat, 112, 142-149
Osnabrück, 21

Paris, 46, 73, 84
Parkin, Sergeant, 20, 35
Pat O'Leary Line, 112, 129, 139
Perignon, 57
Perpignan, 112, 150
Peyaud, 108
Philippe, 97
Pierre, 138, 141
Pierrefiche, Monsieur, 134-136

Pierrefitte-sur-Aire, 50
Poitiers, 106, 120
'P'-Popsie, 23, 28, 36
Pyrenees, 98, 150-158

Radio, T1154 and R1155, 24
Rancourt-sur-Ornain, 81, 86
Ravensbrück concentration
   camp, 110
Revigny, 73, 84
Roullier, Robert, 103-105
Roussel, Monsieur, 84, 94, 95
Royal Air Forces Escaping
   Society, 11, 13, 16, 161
Rue Perronet,127
Rue St Claude, 84, 94
Ruffec, 105, 128
Ruhr (Happy Valley), 25
Rumont village, 45, 47
Rupt devant St Mihiel, 45

Safe houses, 17, 62, 112, 131
St Dizier, 35
St Mihiel, 45, 50
Schräge Musik, 34
Security Police, 125
Smith, Sgt (Smithy), 21, 31, 50
SOE, 110

Spain, 61, 73
Spanish Civil Guards, 159
Spanish guides, 148, 149
Sparks, Cpl, 94
Spiquel, Monique, 127, 128
Squadrons, Nos 76 and 78, 19
Stalagluft III, 20
Stülpnagel, Gen von, 103, 105

Tait, Gp Capt J.B., 19
Theckston, Sgt, 20, 31
Toulouse, 98, 112, 139
Troyon, 55
Turin, 21, 23

Ussat, 148, 149
Uxbridge, 161

Varilhes, 112
Vavincourt, 65, 66
Victor, 130
Vitry-le-François, 73, 86, 90, 92

Wake, Nancy, 146
Wellington bomber, 32
Whiteley, Gp Capt J.R., 20
Whitley aircraft, 21

Yatesbury, 42

Other stories of escape and evasion . . .

Ticket to Freedom

by H.J. Spiller

'You are parcel No 82,' she said laughingly, as Herbert Spiller signed his name in Elvire de Greef's 'visitors' book' beneath all the RAF men who had gone before him over the Pyrenees to freedom, thanks to the Comète escape line. Throughout the Second World War there were many clandestine organizations working to assist Allied servicemen to return to take up arms again. RAF bomber crews came to depend on them as a lifeline to freedom in the event of disaster overtaking them. But the cost was high.

In this book, written by one such RAF evader, he tells how he was successfully helped by the Comète line, and how four French people subsequently met their deaths. Some 160 died serving Comète alone, either by execution or in concentration camps. But the line went on until liberation came, and the links forged between the survivors and their 'guests' are today as strong as ever, and form an important and substantial part of the Entente Cordiale.

Free to Fight Again

RAF escapes and evasions 1940–1945

by Alan W. Cooper

When RAF personnel were forced down in enemy territory, the top priority was to get them back to Britain in order to fly once more against the enemy. It was incumbent on them to attempt to evade or escape from capture. But they could not do it on their own.

After Dunkirk, M19, the department set up in the winter of 1938–9 to look after escape and evasion, immediately set wheels in motion to establish escape lines in occupied territory. But their task would have been impossible without the selfless help of the native people of those countries, heroically disregarding the danger to themselves.

And what of the airmen themselves, the 'parcels' who were, if they were lucky, sent down the line to home, and those less lucky left to rely on their own wits and ingenuity to escape capture? Alan Cooper here recounts, often using their own words, the personal stories of over seventy such evaders and escapers who found their way to freedom, from places as far apart as Norway and the Bay of Bengal. There are stories of hi-jacked aircraft, crossing of crocodile swamps, evasions by camel and coffin, survival in the jungle and brushes with the Gestapo.

Alan Cooper, well known for his aviation books *The Men Who Breached the Dams* and *Bombers over Berlin*, here presents not only stories of thrilling personal adventure but also a tribute to the spirit of resistance that shone through in occupied countries in defiance of oppression.

Colditz Last Stop

Six escapes remembered

by Major Jack Pringle

This is the enthralling true life story of the author's escapes from prisons in Italy, Austria and Germany during the last three and a half years of the Second World War. He tells of his experiences inside, and often outside, eleven prisons ranging from the south of Italy to Czechoslovakia on the border with Poland and finally to Colditz in Saxony.

His partners in his amazing exploits were Alastair Cram, in civilian life an Edinburgh barrister, and the legendary Colonel David Stirling, the founder of the SAS and its military techniques which have achieved spectacular results throughout the world in the post-war years. With Stirling he shared four escapes and life on the run but even more they managed to set up a whole escaping organization within some of the prisons which attempted to hold them captive. This book, in addition, records for the first time the duo's quite extraordinary achievements in working with the Czech resistance from inside a camp in Moravia and with German dissidents from within Colditz.

Major Pringle holds the distinction of being one of the very few officers to receive the MC for his escaping efforts during the war. His escape attempts began immediately after capture while fighting against Rommel's Afrika Korps with the 8th Kings Royal Irish Hussars. He explains how there is nothing quite like being on the run, hunted by the enemy, often alone and with the odds always against you.